"We're Just Friends" and Other Dating Lies
Practical Wisdom for Healthy Relationships

Chuck Milian

New
Growth
Press

www.newgrowthpress.com

New Growth Press, Greensboro, NC 27429
Copyright © 2011 by Charles E. Milian. All rights reserved.
Published 2011.

Cover Design: Wendy W. Lam

Typesetting: Lisa Parnell, Thompson's Station, TN

ISBN-13: 978-1-935273-83-7
ISBN-10: 1-935273-83-3

Library of Congress Cataloging-in-Publication Data
Milian, Charles E. (Charles Edward), 1961–
    "We're just friends" and other dating lies : practical wisdom for healthy
relationships / Charles E. Milian.
        p. cm.
    Includes bibliographical references and index.
    ISBN-13: 978-1-935273-83-7 (alk. paper)
    ISBN-10: 1-935273-83-3 (alk. paper)
    1. Single people—Conduct of life. 2. Dating (Social customs)—
Religious aspects—Christianity. 3. Friendship—Religious aspects—
Christianity. I. Title.
    BV4596.S5M55 2011
    241'.6765—dc22   2010023303

Printed in Canada

18 17 16 15 14 13 12 11   2 3 4 5

Contents

Foreword

Whenever I offer dating advice to my 30-year-old daughter, she reminds me that it's been a long time since I was "out there." She's right, of course. But while dating patterns and expectations have changed, some things remain the same. Dating is still a process through which young people in our culture select their mates. And dating still is an experience that leaves many wounded and confused.

Pastor Chuck Milian doesn't want to rob dating of romance or mystery. But he does want to protect dating couples from unnecessary hurt and tragic choices. Our society puts tremendous dating pressure on both men and women—pressures that are intensified by unrealistic expectations and what Chuck calls "dating lies." So in this book Pastor Chuck presents a framework for dating that relieves many of the pressures, and encourages the development of truly healthy Christian relationships.

The framework for dating that Milian presents is rooted in a profound understanding of Scripture, cross-cultural research in male/female relationships, and many years of counseling individuals and couples. Within the framework of what the author calls dating "levels," Chuck deals with issue after issue, from appropriate physical contact to how to end a relationship without hurting the other person. With insight and sensitivity Pastor Chuck looks at some of the "lies" (false expectations) that make dating a minefield, and he shows dating couples how to keep on the same page with their feelings and expectations.

Chuck rightly emphasizes the importance of a supportive community as a relational safety net. While he shows how an individual can share the principles imbedded in this book with his or her date, the greatest value of the book is as a guide to those ministering to youth and young adults. Teaching his strategy for dating so that it is understood and practiced by a community of teens or adults can make dating a positive adventure, free of the wounds and embarrassment that so often are a part of dating today.

I heartily recommend this book to individuals, and especially to those in ministry. What a wonderful tool for teaching a thoroughly Christian and healthy way to date!

Larry Richards, Ph.D.

Acknowledgments

First and foremost, I want to give thanks and glory to my Lord and Savior Jesus Christ who saved me by his loving and gracious sacrifice on the cross of Calvary. He pursued me even in my rebellion, revealed himself to me, received me, washed me, filled me, guided me, and has continued to bless me even up to this very moment. Anything good in this book is because of him.

A big thank you is also in order for several special people who have walked through this book-writing journey with me. I am deeply grateful for their love, support, feedback, and encouragement.

To my wife Kim who, besides Jesus, is the best thing that ever happened to me. Thank you, Honey, for helping me to press on with this and for patiently helping me begin to understand things from a woman's perspective. I love you!

To my two sons, Josh and Caleb, who continually encouraged me along the way. I'm so proud of you both and know God has great things in store for you.

To the wonderful people at Crossroads Fellowship, I am so thankful to be your pastor and to share life's journey with you as we seek to reach our city for Christ.

To everyone on the team at New Growth Press, without whom this book would not have happened.

Introduction

Tell me if this sounds familiar. You're at a social gathering with the person you have been dating for the past six months. Someone asks you, "Are you two getting serious?" and your partner quickly responds, "Oh, we're just friends." *Just friends?!* Six months of multiple dates each week, talking on the phone several times a day, sharing personal struggles and dreams, kissing (and perhaps more), and *we're just friends?!* Or maybe you have found yourself on the other side of the expectations gap. You've been on a few dates with a person. Things are going fine, but it's nothing serious. At least you thought it was nothing serious until you hear from a friend who heard from a friend who heard from your "partner" that you might be "the one."

Of all human relationships, dating relationships are some of the hardest to navigate. An already difficult endeavor is made even worse by ever-changing social norms, unruly physical desires, and unrealistic images of what relationships should look like. But perhaps the greatest challenge is conflicting expectations. We just don't know what to expect when it comes to dating.

In earlier times and in other parts of the world, the path toward marriage was and is more clearly marked out than it is today in Western culture. Whether or not we approve of arranged marriages or old-fashioned courtship rituals, we have to give them this: they make it a lot easier to manage expectations and help ensure that everybody is on the same page. But you don't have to ascribe to these systems to realize that managing your expectations, as well as those of the people you date, would make dating much better. Being able to line up your relationship expectations with your commitments will help you to better understand how to think, feel, and act in the context of a dating relationship.

Someone once said, "If you don't know where you are going, you might wind up someplace else." Do you ever feel like you don't know where you're going in your dating relationships? Or perhaps you know where you want to be going, but you can't see how to get there. For many singles in our culture, dating is a vast, uncharted wilderness that they get dropped off in sometime after puberty—good luck finding the trail!

I have good news for you. You are currently standing at the trailhead, and there is a clearly marked trail in front of you. There is a way of dating that I call the Five Dating Levels, and it actually works. The goal of this system is to allow you to have fun, develop good relationships, avoid unnecessary hurts, know "where you are" each step of the way, and know when and if you should move forward. Ultimately, I hope to show you a clear, easy, and relatively safe way to date, which will work for you and anyone else who is willing to embrace God's design for relationships.

CHAPTER ONE

The Five Dating Levels

Dating Lie #1: Love just happens; you can't control it.

Christians spend a lot of time and energy trying to understand how to be more like Christ. Why is it then that the way we date looks so much like the way the world dates? I'm not just talking about sexual matters. Hopefully single Christians know better than to take at face value the sex advice offered in magazines such as *Cosmopolitan* and *Esquire*. But even if you do show more sexual restraint than the couple in the most recent romantic comedy, do you also resist the world's idea of what dating is for? Do you look at dating mostly as a means of getting what you want for yourself? Are you expecting a romantic partner to define who you are? Does "failure" in the dating arena make you feel like there is something wrong with you?

The fact that the divorce rate among professing Christians is the same as the divorce rate for everybody else (about 50 percent) suggests that our view of male-female relationships hasn't been transformed

> Even if you do show more sexual restraint than the couple in the most recent romantic comedy, do you also resist the world's idea of what dating is for?

as fully as it needs to be. That's a problem. Our culture is out of sync with the reality of how healthy relationships actually develop. The result is broken hearts, ruined friendships, bitterness, and a lack of commitment. We have abandoned or forgotten some universal truths that are not only wise but extremely practical. In essence, we have taken an off-ramp from the highway of healthy relational development. This off-ramp is a wrong exit; it cannot lead us to our desired destination.

Let me tell a story about a Christian friend of mine who, for all his great qualities, still dated according to the world's standards. He was a good-looking guy, had a great personality, owned his own business, came from a good family, was on fire for the Lord, was active in serving others, and had leadership gifts. By all typical definitions, he was a "great catch" for any of the hundreds of single women in our singles ministry. As a result, he dated many of these women, but he quickly developed a reputation as an unpredictable and confusing heartbreaker. Women began to avoid him, his relationships suffered, and his witness was damaged.

The women complained that he confused them with his words and actions. For example, he would say very flattering things, which he believed, but were really not appropriate for where they were in the relationship. He often would stay up late with them talking about topics that were too emotional for their level of commitment. He also would arrange an excessive number of activities during the first month of dating, which didn't allow any time to gain perspective on the relationship. Kissing and lots of physical contact also began almost immediately, which made the women feel like he was exclusively interested in them. When they found out that he was doing the same thing with other women at the same time, or when he abruptly ended the relationship, they were deeply hurt and confused. There were even some interpersonal conflicts among the other members of the singles ministry because of his behavior. A few women began to take sides against each other, feeling like the other women had unfairly barged in on what they thought was a unique and special relationship. Gossip began and some women even felt so embarrassed and uncomfortable that they considered no longer attending the group. Several of the men felt like this guy was trying to create a harem and was manipulatively taking multiple women out of circulation in order to eliminate competition. As this story demonstrates, without clear parameters and expectations, even the Christian community can sink to the lowest levels of humanity and suffer severe damage. Unfortunately, this story is not unique.

If not for two things, this young man's life could have taken a very negative turn. He could have become discouraged, felt isolated, and wandered back into the world from which he had recently escaped. First, he was approached by a godly Christian counselor who had talked with several of the women he had hurt. The counselor lovingly confronted him about the negative impact he was having on the singles community and his own personal testimony as a believer. He patiently explained how and why the young man's dating habits were causing such pain and confusion. Second, this man had the courage to share all of this with his small group. This group of men, who were committed to helping each other become fully devoted followers of Christ, began holding their friend accountable and challenging him on his destructive dating habits. They all knew that he was ignorant of the Bible's view of healthy interactions between men and women. They also knew that transformation is a process that requires time and practice as well as support from others willing to encourage progress and speak the truth in love about failings.

This man was convicted by the Lord that he needed to go back to the women he had hurt and confess his sins, ask for forgiveness, and then reestablish his reputation as a trustworthy man of God by dating well from that point forward. Though this was a very difficult and painful process, he had the humility to do the right thing, trusting that God would ultimately bring great blessing out of his obedience. As he grew in understanding about communication, boundaries, commitment levels, and the process of intimacy development, he not only developed a reputation as a godly man but also as a safe, fun, and desirable man to date. From that point forward any woman he dated was protected, encouraged in Christ, and treated with the utmost respect. Ultimately, God used this experience to prepare him for a relationship with a wonderful woman who would later become his wife. Nineteen years of marriage and two kids later, this couple has an enviable marriage that has been a blessing to them and to hundreds of others. True to the Lord's sense of irony, God has used this man to teach and counsel countless younger men to live, date, and marry in healthy and productive ways.

There are many points that could be taken from that story, but I want to focus on two in particular. First, we all play a part in a complicated web of relationships. It was bad enough that my friend's dysfunctional attitude toward dating hurt the women he dated, but he also hurt other people in his relational web. Just within our singles group, there were those who felt the need to take sides in the romantic dramas he started. There were the men who later dated the women he had broken up with. There was the gossip that caused any number of people to stumble. Seeing the pervasive relational fallout that can result from bad dating practices emphasizes why it is so important to seek God's wisdom as we seek intimate relationships. Second, this story demonstrates that it's never too late to change. Whatever your history, God honors your efforts to walk in a way that is pleasing to him.

There is no reason why it shouldn't be possible for a dating relationship to end well if time and interaction reveal that a couple is not well suited for marriage. What does it mean to "end well"? It means you can look a person you used to date in the eye without pain or awkwardness. It means you can pray for that person—pray that his or her life will be blessed and happy without you. It means you have dated in such a way that the worst thing that can happen is that you have built a friendship that you can retain, even after one or both of you gets married to somebody else. That's not just wishful thinking.

An Overview of the Five Dating Levels

I've been in full-time ministry for more than twenty-two years, and for twenty of those years, I've been a pastor in a large church in North Carolina. I've performed over a hundred and fifty weddings and counseled countless couples about how to date well, how to move forward, when to not move forward, and how to be happily married. As I talked with people and helped them wrestle through the confusion of emotions and expectations of dating, it became apparent that we all need a clear, simple, realistic, and biblical way to navigate this thing called dating. I studied the Scripture, considered my own imperfect past, read research from Christian counselors, and even gleaned insights from the sciences of zoology and anthropology. What emerged from my study and prayer was the Five Dating Levels.

I've developed a system that categorizes dating relationships based on their level of commitment, progressing from lowest to highest. In fact, the highest level is dating in the context of marriage (you did know that dating continues after marriage, didn't you?). The Five Dating Levels gives you a plan for relating to the opposite sex in a dating relationship that is based on first loving God and then others.

God says that a man is to leave his family and be united with his wife to form a new family (Genesis 2:24). As I mentioned earlier, in other cultures and times there were clearer guidelines to help this process of leaving and cleaving. While our culture treats this process as a free-for-all, the Five Dating Levels offers a way to bring wisdom and structure to this important life stage. This dating system takes Paul's plea to consider others' interests before our own and applies it directly to dating relationships (Philippians 2:4).

Below you'll find a diagram of the system and a summary description of each level. We'll get into a lot more detail later, but this should give you a good idea of where we're headed.

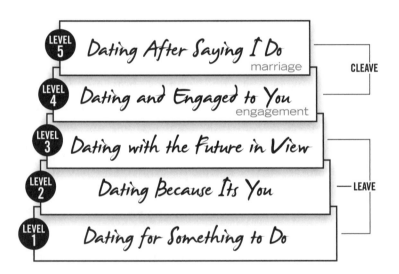

LEVEL ONE: DATING FOR SOMETHING TO DO

This can be a onetime date or one of many "getting to know you better" events. No physical contact should occur at this level. Preferably, a Level One date is a group event. Absolutely no obligation to continue dating exists afterward on either person's part.

LEVEL TWO: DATING BECAUSE IT'S YOU

This is still not an exclusive relationship, but it does require one or both people to acknowledge a true interest or attraction that has grown over time. No kissing should occur at this level. Level Two dates should be mostly group events with some time spent alone. An obligation exists on each person's part to communicate honestly and clearly about how he or she is feeling along the way.

LEVEL THREE: DATING WITH THE FUTURE IN VIEW

This is an exclusive relationship. Kissing can begin at this level but is to be avoided if it stirs too much passion. There should be an equal division between time alone and time with groups for accountability and perspective. As always, both the man and the woman should communicate openly and honestly along the way. The focus is on clarifying life goals and true compatibility.

LEVEL FOUR: DATING AND ENGAGED TO YOU

On this level, the focus is on clarifying roles, family boundaries, premarital counseling, and planning life together. Physical limits may need extra protection as desires will increase with commitments.

LEVEL FIVE: DATING AFTER SAYING I DO

After marriage, sexual intimacy brings a whole new dimension to the relationship. Weekly dates are critical to keep romance alive, maintain open communication, and mature the relationship so that it is prepared for possible children and eventual empty nest syndrome.

The Five Dating Levels are a progression toward wholeness and holiness. Each level is designed to develop an appropriate degree of bonding, which makes it possible for the relationship to handle the weight and stress of the next level without being crushed. The limits established at each level protect the relationship from going where it shouldn't go. But progressing to the next level is not the only purpose of this process. Hopefully, at each stage you will notice and experience the God-designed gift that is specific to that level. It is also worth noting that the "rules and regulations" of the Five Dating Levels aren't intended to squelch intimacy. Instead they should create a safe environment where healthy dating and true intimacy can take place. People don't date when they don't feel safe, and safety is what fosters true intimacy. Isn't intimacy what we're looking for when we date?

Physical Boundaries

Each dating level represents a level of commitment that should be accompanied by appropriate physical and emotional boundaries. What should you be doing? What should you be feeling? What is appropriate to devote your mental energies to? What plans should you be making? Most of this book is devoted to answering those questions.

Admittedly, there is a lot that is mysterious in attraction and love, but thankfully God's Word, human experience, and even scientific research reveal a clear design in relational development. This design points to practical things we can do to greatly increase our chances of being happy in our relationships. It also clearly shows us what *not* to do.

Obviously, there are cultural factors that influence the way we understand the physical relationships between men and women. You don't often see a man kissing a woman's hand these days. In other cultures, ideas of modesty are different from ours. Nevertheless, there are universal standards that govern the way men and women relate to one another physically.

In his book *Bonding*, Dr. Donald Joy discusses a remarkable anthropological study that discovered twelve "bonding stages."[1] These stages mark the development of relationships between men and women—from less intimate contact to more intimate contact—across all human cultures. As diverse as human cultures are, and as different as their sexual mores can be, these stages seem to be the normal progression of physical contact throughout the world. In fact, the study didn't find any culture where it was normal for a man to put his arm around a woman's waist before he put his arm around her shoulder, or where it was normal for a man to touch a woman's face if he had never touched her hand. While there are abundant examples of *individuals* who ignore or skip steps in this progression, the point is that these stages are the *norm*.

When these stages are respected and followed, Joy argues, the result is healthy relationships and a stable society. However, when these stages are ignored, skipped, or rushed through, the result is a marked increase in violent sexual behavior, dysfunctional bonds, and broken marriages. Many other social ills flow out of this type of environment as well, such as increased poverty, crime, and isolation. You only need to read the front page of any newspaper in America to see the proof of this research. If we're going to establish physical boundaries for the Five Dating Levels, the Twelve Bonding Stages seem like a good place to start. The chart below lists the Twelve Bonding Stages and shows how they map on to the Five Dating Levels.

Dating Level	Physical Boundaries	Basic Description of Interaction
Level 1: Dating for Something to Do	1. Eye-to-Body 2. Eye-to-Eye 3. Voice-to-Voice	This can be a onetime date or one of many "getting to know you better" events. There is no physical contact allowed, preferably a group event, and no obligation exists afterward on either person's part. **The risk level is low.**
Level 2: Dating Because It's You	4. Hand-to-Hand 5. Arm-to-Shoulder 6. Arm-to-Waist	This is still not an exclusive relationship but does require one or both people to acknowledge a true interest or attraction that has grown over time. There is no kissing allowed; it should be mostly group events with some time alone. An obligation exists on both persons' parts to communicate honestly and clearly about how they are feeling along the way. **The risk level is medium.**
Level 3: Dating with the Future in View	7. Face-to-Face 8. Hand-to-Head 9. Hand-to-Body	This is an exclusive relationship. Kissing begins at this level but is to be avoided if it stirs too much passion. Equal time alone & with groups for accountability and perspective. An obligation exists to communicate openly and honestly along the way. The focus is on clarifying life goals and true compatibility. **The risk level is high.**

Level 4: Dating and Engaged to You	No Physical Progression… "a Holy Pause"	Focus is on clarifying roles, family boundaries, premarital counseling, and planning life together. Physical limits may need extra protection as desires will increase with commitments.
Level 5: Dating After Saying I Do	10. Mouth-to- Breast 11. Hand-to-Genital 12. Genital-to- Genital	After marriage, sexual intimacy brings a whole new dimension to the relationship. Weekly dates are critical to keep romance alive, maintain open communication, and mature the relationship so that it is prepared for possible children and eventual 'empty nest syndrome'.

At times my guidelines may look like a mere list of rules, but you'll miss the point if you get stuck here. The point is to set expectations that will serve as signposts that tell you (1) where you should be now; (2) what the next level should look like; (3) whether to stay where you are, move to the next level, or call it quits. When two people have kept their personal interactions and perspectives consistent with the level of their personal commitments, they can part ways without seriously wounding one another.

Remember, these are guidelines that need to be applied with wisdom and shouldn't be used legalistically. The point is to honor God by honoring his design for interaction between men and women. Using these

> When two people have kept their personal interactions and perspectives consistent with the level of their personal commitments, they can part ways without seriously wounding one another.

guidelines is one way to protect against becoming emotionally and sexually intimate too soon. It's a practical way to put the best interests of the people you date before your own selfish desires.

If Dating Were Like Going to the Mall

Before moving on, let me offer a quick analogy to further clarify how the levels function. Think of the Five Dating Levels as the levels of a five-story mall. Within this very big and very complex structure it would be easy to get lost. Thankfully, wherever you are in the mall, you're never too far from one of those kiosks with a map that says "YOU ARE HERE" to help you find your way around.

It would be great if dating was a little more like that—if both you and the person you were dating always knew exactly where you were. You and a member of the opposite sex enter the mall at the ground level, stop at the directory, and get your bearings. You casually stroll along and enjoy the activity of seeing what comes your way. The topics of conversation are at first determined by the people you pass or the things you see in the windows. Together you enter stores that appeal to one or the other of you, stores displaying items of personal interest. This enables you to learn about each other by discovering what the other is interested in. You see which magazines your date leafs through in the bookstore. Your date sees which section of the sporting goods store catches your eye.

After a while—if you both agree you're ready—the two of you go up the escalator to the second level, where the items on display are a little more personal and allow for deeper levels of sharing. Over the course of time, you return to the mall week after week, month after month, eventually daring to go up escalator after escalator until you reach the fourth level of the mall where you enter the jewelry store! As you pick out an engagement ring, you gaze up to the fifth and final level into the maternity shop, and you wonder how much longer before that store will be your destination.

That's what the Five Dating Levels looks like. It keeps things casual at first, ensuring that nobody feels any pressure to make any commitment, and that nobody is doing or saying anything that implies a commitment that isn't there. Just as importantly, the Five Dating Levels provides a dating couple with the sign-posts to know when it is time to go to the next level, where the commitments are greater and intimacy increases both emotionally and physically. But how do you navigate that process? How do you know when it's time to "go up the escalator"? To answer these questions you must maintain a healthy Truth Triangle, which is the topic of the next chapter.

CHAPTER TWO

Introducing the Truth Triangle

Dating Lie #2: If it feels like love, it must be love.

As I mentioned, rules are a part of the Five Dating Levels, but that's not essentially what they are about. The guidelines I offer are about keeping your thoughts, feelings, and behaviors in balance and are based on the foundation of your commitment to the person (or persons) you're dating. I like to illustrate that balance with a diagram I call the Truth Triangle.

A healthy Truth Triangle is an equilateral triangle, which means it's balanced. One of the main reasons people have problems in their dating relationships is because what they *say* and *do* (behavior) doesn't match what they have been allowing themselves to *think* and *feel*. A healthy Truth Triangle is also the appropriate size. What determines how long each side of the triangle should be is your commitment level. As your level of commitment grows, the sides of your Truth Triangle grow. You can let yourself think more

One of the main reasons people have problems in their dating relationships is because what they **say** and **do** (behavior) doesn't match what they have been allowing themselves to **think** and **feel**.

seriously, feel more deeply, and behave more intimately (within well-defined limits) as you and the person you date agree to be more committed.

When one or more elements of the Truth Triangle are out of alignment, it won't be long before confusion, misunderstandings, and broken hearts abound. For example, if your feelings run ahead of your thinking and behaviors, your Truth Triangle will look like this:

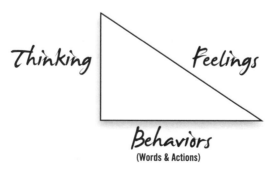

17

Allowing feelings of love and passion to flow before they have been proven accurate by months of time spent interacting is extremely unwise. Notice that when your feelings get out of whack, your behaviors get out of whack too. When you are swept away by your feelings, you're in danger of doing and saying things that don't line up with your commitments. These untested feelings cannot be trusted!

If your thinking is not consistent with your feelings and behaviors, your Truth Triangle will look like this:

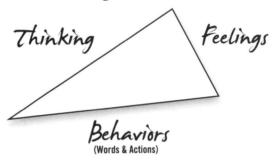

Spending your time thinking about "a future together" or imagining what it would be like to be married before the relationship has been proven over time is equally unwise. Again, behaviors get out of whack as your thinking gets out of whack. Just as you can be swept away by your feelings, you can also rationalize behaviors that are inappropriate. These unsubstantiated thoughts cannot be trusted!

If your behavior is not consistent with your feelings and thinking, your Truth Triangle will look like this:

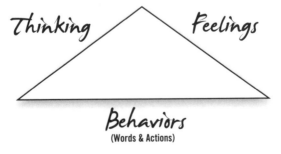

Behaviors such as kissing (before Level Three), spending too much time together too soon, and saying I love you before the relationship has had enough time to properly form are also unwise. Just as unsubstantiated thoughts and untested feelings can lead you to inappropriate behaviors, inappropriate behaviors can affect the things you (and the person you're dating) think and feel. It works both ways. These unacceptable and selfish behaviors cannot be allowed to go unchecked!

> When your feelings get out of whack, your behaviors get out of whack too. When you are swept away by your feelings, you're in danger of doing and saying things that don't line up with your commitments. These untested feelings cannot be trusted!

Rebalancing Your Truth Triangle

God has the same expectations for holiness for men as he has for women, which makes the Truth Triangle equally relevant for both. But, in most cases, men and women struggle differently with keeping the Truth Triangle balanced. Typically, men don't keep their behaviors in check, while women tend to let their feelings get out of control.

When it comes to living in the world of feelings, women are much more at home than men. They naturally feel their feelings in a way that men simply don't. That's not to say that men don't have feelings, but that they aren't usually in touch with their feelings like women are. For a woman, even if her feelings have led her down the wrong path, they can still be the key to getting her back on track. Feelings don't come out of nowhere. The following is a helpful tool to discover where they come from:

What you *feel* is based on what you *think*.
What you *think* is based on what you *believe*.
What you *believe* is either *true* or *false*.

What is the significance of that feelings-thoughts-beliefs pathway? For one thing, it gives you a way of evaluating what you feel. All feelings are real: you feel what you feel. But not all feelings are based on reality.

> Men and women struggle differently with keeping the Truth Triangle balanced. Typically, men don't keep their behaviors in check, while women tend to let their feelings get out of control.

When a woman is trying to get her Truth Triangle in balance, she has to ask, "What am I feeling?" This is valuable because it is the best way for her to discover what she is thinking. And once she understands what she is thinking, she can compare those thoughts to what she knows to be the truth. Do your thoughts and feelings and behaviors line up with the truth? Do they line up with your level of commitment?

Men usually have to take a slightly different approach. Because men typically don't know what they're feeling, trying to pinpoint thought patterns this way is usually ineffective. I advise men to start with their behaviors. That's where men live: not in the world of emotions, but the world of actions. I urge men to focus on their behaviors while they wrestle with God. If they can get their behaviors under control—if they can line up the things they say and the commitments they have made—they can begin to get their thoughts and feelings under control.

CHAPTER THREE

What a Date Is *Not*!

Dating Lie #3: Think of every date as a potential mate.

This book primarily is about what dating *is,* or at least, *should be.* But before we dive into defining and exploring what a real date is, we should understand well what a date is *not.* Much of the trouble people experience in their dating lives comes down to a basic misunderstanding of what this new relationship should look like.

The Five Dating Levels seek to redefine dating instead of using the world's definition. For example, what our culture usually calls a first date would fall somewhere around Level Two or Three. The purpose of this system is to scale back the pressure of dating and give you a nice, easy way to enter into a dating relationship. Despite what the world may say, below are four things that a date is definitely *not.*

1. A date is *not* a commitment to marriage, a relationship, or even another date

While this may seem obvious, far too often, after the equivalent of a Level One date, friends and family will ask questions that would be embarrassing if your date heard them. Unchecked, our minds tend to race ahead, playing out scenarios before we've even completed the first date. This pseudo reality puts far too much pressure on both parties and is the reason many people today are hesitant to ask for a simple date. The beauty of the Dating Levels (especially Level One) is that it removes all the pressure from unrealistic expectations and allows the freedom to simply have fun with as many different people as desired. This variety of inter-action helps you learn what you like in a potential partner and what you don't. It also helps you learn about yourself and become more realistic and accepting of other imperfect people—a critical component for a happy and lasting marriage!

> Variety of interaction helps you learn what you like in a potential partner and what you don't. It also helps you learn about yourself and become more realistic and accepting of other imperfect people—a critical component for a happy and lasting marriage!

2. A date is *not* a vehicle for meeting sexual desires

"For this reason a man will leave his father and mother and be united to his wife, and they will become one flesh. The man and his wife were both naked, and they felt no shame" (Genesis 2:24–25). From the very beginning, God makes it clear that our sexual desires are only to be met in marriage. Only as a man and a woman cleave to one another in a committed relation-ship under God's authority can they become one flesh without feeling shame. Paul exhorts us to treat the opposite sex with purity, as if they were family members: "Treat younger men as brothers, older women as mothers, and younger women as sisters, with absolute purity" (1 Timothy 5:1–2). It seems that each generation must learn the same lessons over again. The old-fashioned values of the older generation are initially rejected by the youth and only accepted as true much later, after unnecessary suffering has occurred. A large part of this journey is young men learning how to treat young women as sisters and not objects—a completely counter-cultural perspective.

During my teens and early twenties, my perception of what I saw on television, heard on the radio, or observed with the people around me indicated that sexual expression outside of marriage (i.e., on a date) was not only acceptable, but normal. Unfortunately, what I perceived was a lie. Despite modern culture's permissiveness regarding this issue, the internal and universal design of human beings functions best when it is aligned with the Bible's teachings that reserve purity and sexual expression for marriage. Not only does society function better when the biblical parameters are followed, but couples tend to report a much higher satisfaction and fulfillment in their relationships as well.

The highest and most complete experience of intimacy for human beings is *not* simple sexual union; it occurs when there is a consistent and harmonious interaction of spiritual unity, emotional oneness, intellectual stimulation, and relational security over a long period of time. This interaction leads a man and a woman to commit officially and publicly to be united and monogamous for life, and to seal their commitment with the final phase of bonding called sexual intimacy. Obviously, this reality undermines the present cultural trends of casual sex and "safe foreplay" as acceptable dating behaviors. The sad evidence seen in our high divorce rate and climbing rates of sexually transmitted diseases[2] is overwhelming proof that dating is an activity which requires purity in our actions toward one another.

3. A date is *not* a vehicle for building your social status

> Therefore, I urge you, brothers, in view of God's mercy, to offer your bodies as living sacrifices, holy and pleasing to God—this is your spiritual act of worship. *Do not conform any longer to the pattern of this world*, but be transformed by the renewing of your mind. Then you will be able to test and approve what God's will is—his good, pleasing and perfect will...*Love must be sincere.* Hate what is evil; cling to what is good. Be devoted to one another in brotherly love. *Honor one another above yourselves.* (Romans 12:1–2, 9–10, emphasis added)

These verses from Romans are a call to resist the cultural norm of devaluing other people in order to get what you want. We are to reject conformity to a self-centered worldview and treat one another with sincere love, respect, and purity. Surprisingly, many people view dating and ultimately marriage as a means for improving their social status or joining a higher socioeconomic level. While many point to certain financial hardships or limitations created by gender bias as justification for these relationships of convenience, this type of thinking is absolutely contrary to God's design for relationships and counterproductive to the basic human need for love.

4. A date is *not* a statement of your value as a person

Because of the present crisis, I think that it is good for you to remain as you are. Are you married? Do not seek a divorce. Are you unmarried? Do not look for a wife. But if you do marry, you have not sinned; and if a virgin marries, she has not sinned. But those who marry will face many troubles in this life, and I want to spare you this. (1 Corinthians 7:26–28)

Your marital status has nothing to do with your value as a person. Many foolishly rush into unhealthy marriages simply because they believe the lie that singleness is a curse and proof that they are rejects.

> It was for you that Jesus endured the cross. How can a date—or even a marriage—give you a higher status than that?

Others made the same mistake simply because their biological clocks were ticking and they were getting older.

Don't look to your dating track record if you want to know who you are. Look at who Scripture says you are: you are the "joy set before" Jesus: "Let us fix our eyes on Jesus, the author and perfecter of our faith, who for the joy set before him endured the cross, scorning its shame, and sat down at the right hand of the throne of God" (Hebrews 12:2). It was for you that Jesus endured the cross. How can a date—or even a marriage—give you a higher status than that? How can a rejection or a bad breakup really take anything away from a person who is that valued by Christ? Doing the right thing relationally will sometimes feel like "death on a cross" (Philippians 2:8). Commit yourself to Jesus, who has already suffered this for you, and you will be amazed at the power you have to be relationally healthy.

My Story

Prior to my conversion to Jesus Christ, I dated according to what I had seen and read in popular culture. The results I got were proof that I was out of sync with relational reality. Not only were my methods, expectations, and attitudes unrealistic, but my own personal baggage sabotaged even my best efforts. To put it bluntly, I carelessly let physical attraction be the primary driver in forming relationships, and I ended up dating a lot of women with whom I was not compatible. I also found that this one-dimensional approach led me to relationships with women who could be very spiteful and self-centered. Almost without exception these relationships became inappropriately physical, ended badly, and many people (including myself) were deeply hurt.

One of the mistakes I made was rushing. A magical moment on the dance floor of a bar would lead to a night in my apartment, and the physical connection would be misunderstood as a relationship. I found myself in many multi-month relationships with women I didn't really like, especially the more I got to know them. For those few relationships where there was some level of compatibility, and we were together for a year or more, some significant dysfunction (alcoholism, abuse, family problems, or codependency) always undermined us as a couple.

A lot of the responsibility for this painful journey rests with me. I had significant esteem issues due to some painful events in my childhood, and not having a relationship with God, I had no idea about who I was in Christ. I projected my fears and misconceptions on the people around me. I vacillated between being a nice doormat to being self-centered and determined never to be hurt by anyone again. I made sure that if hurting was going to happen, I would be giving and not receiving. My attraction grid was distorted and blurred by sin, and I found myself continuously dating the same person with a different name and face. I was stuck in a dysfunctional rut and didn't even know it.

All of this was happening amidst great worldly success. I was the president of my high school, played varsity football, made the honor roll, and was given a high level of authority and position at my job despite my inexperience. I was driven, had plenty of people I called friends, and was considered good-looking. But none of this stopped the woeful emptiness

I felt inside, or my complete inability to have a healthy and committed relationship.

After my conversion, I began to deal with my personal baggage and reject the methods of popular culture. I was able to get on a healthy path, and I can testify to the power and positive impact of God's relational design. It wouldn't make me uncomfortable to be around any woman I dated after my conversion. There is no embarrassment and no old wounds. In fact, when I got married, our wedding party included the last girl I dated before I met my wife. She married one of my good friends, and I was a groomsman in their wedding.

By aligning myself with the relational design of our Creator, I was able to not only date and marry well, but also to protect our community of friendships from harm. Not long ago, one of my accountability partners was a man whom my wife dated seriously before we were married. Can you imagine sharing your dreams, struggles, weaknesses, and daily journey with someone who once held the affection of your spouse? This is neither weird nor impossible; it is the way things work when relationships are done biblically.

Only God can make this kind of healthy interaction possible. The world longs for this type of safety, clarity, and healthy community. As believers, we can show them the way, but we have to be willing to travel against the tide of culture and get back on the road of relational reality—by following God's design.

You are a part of God's plan; that doesn't depend on your marital status or your dating life. "For we are God's workmanship, created in Christ Jesus to do good works, which God prepared in advance for us to do" (Ephesians 2:10). This is one of my favorite Bible verses because it clearly tells us that God made us, has a plan for us, and has ordained things for us to do. We are part of his master plan. This means that every person you date should be drawn closer to God and strengthened spiritually because of their interaction with you—that is God's plan!

Countless singles struggle with feelings of inadequacy due to our cultural misunderstandings about marriage. The Bible makes it clear that staying single is okay with God—Jesus was single. The apostle Paul appears to have been either single or single again as a widower. Despite this fact, many singles dread the weekends when the dates they were hoping for do not materialize. They mourn the lost opportunities and dread the questions that unthinking people might ask. Over time, they improperly internalize these feelings and begin to devalue themselves, feeling like second-class citizens. Your value as a person comes from the fact that God himself created you uniquely for his pleasure. He died on that cross for you because of the joy he had when he looked into the future and saw you in his kingdom. You have a purpose in this life that no one else can fulfill. These truths and nothing else determine a person's value. With that in mind, let's take a quick detour to talk about singleness. After all, every dating relationship starts with two single people!

INTERLUDE
Being Single

I know what you're thinking: "Singleness? I sat down to read a book about dating, not about being single!" Sorry. This isn't the old switcheroo, I promise. It's just that if you don't get singleness right, you aren't going to get dating right either.

All of your dating relationships except one will end and leave you single. That means at least two things: First, you should be sure you know how to end a dating relationship well (that's a topic we'll cover later). Second, you should be sure you have a biblical view of singleness.

CHAPTER FOUR

A Biblical View of Singleness

Dating Lie #4: If you're single, you're incomplete.

Some of the greatest leaders in church history lived their whole lives as singles: Saint Francis of Assisi, Thomas Aquinas, Joan of Arc, Teresa of Avila, Thomas à Kempis, Bernard of Clairvaux. More recently, Protestant leaders such as Methodist circuit rider Francis Asbury, missionaries Amy Carmichael and Helen Roseveare, and German martyr Dietrich Bonhoeffer were all single. C. S. Lewis was a bachelor for most of his life, married at age fifty-seven, was married for only four years, and remained a celibate widower after his wife's death. British theologian John Stott, now in his seventies and never married, has had a significant worldwide ministry. Mother Teresa spent seven decades serving the poor in India as a single woman.[3]

Contrary to what any misguided relative may say to you, there is nothing wrong with being single. In fact, God says it is a gift from him! Paul wrote to the Corinthians,

> I wish that all men were as I am. But each man has his own gift from God; one has this gift, another has that. Now to the unmarried and the widows I say: It is good for them to stay unmarried, as I am. But if they cannot

control themselves, they should marry, for it is better to marry than to burn with passion. (1 Corinthians 7:7–9)

Neither marriage nor singleness is a sin; both are gifts from God.

Three Unbiblical Views of Singleness

Despite singleness being as much a gift as marriage in God's eyes, three unbiblical views of singleness persist. Worst of all, these three views tend to be most persistent in the minds of people who are single but wish they weren't.

UNBIBLICAL VIEW #1: IF YOU ARE SINGLE, GOD IS PUNISHING YOU FOR PAST SINS

In this view, you tend to wallow in shame or rail in anger at God. Neither reaction has any positive or redemptive results. You are a prisoner of your own misunderstanding because you do not know Scripture.

> Neither marriage nor singleness is a sin; both are gifts from God.

If we claim to be without sin, we deceive ourselves and the truth is not in us. If we confess our sins, he is faithful and just and will forgive us our sins and purify us from all unrighteousness. If we claim we have not sinned, we make him out to be a liar and his word has no place in our lives. (1 John 1:8–10)

If you have received Christ, God doesn't need to punish you for your sins because Jesus took the punishment already. Jesus is "faithful and just" (in other words, he is able) to forgive and cleanse you. This means your singleness is *not* a punishment from God!

UNBIBLICAL VIEW #2: IF YOU ARE SINGLE, YOU ARE INCOMPLETE AND DOOMED TO A LESSER LIFE

In this view, you tend to struggle with a sense of helplessness because you can't make someone marry you. You're angry with others and feel doomed to miss out on all the best things in life. While it is true that if you never marry some aspects of life will not be yours to experience (being a parent, for example), this in no way means that your are sentenced to a dull life or a lack of purpose and meaning. Ask Mother Teresa.

"For we are God's workmanship, created in Christ Jesus to do good works, which God prepared in advance for us to do" (Ephesians 2:10). If you are single right now, it is part of God's purpose. Only he knows your future, but if you focus on the present and you accept your singleness as part of his plan, then you can get on with living a full life knowing you are at the center of his will. He'll take care of tomorrow; live fully devoted to him today! Furthermore, it's not just that God has a plan for you. He has a good plan. "'For I know the plans I have for you,' declares the LORD, 'plans to prosper you and not to harm you, plans to give you hope and a future'" (Jeremiah 29:11). Whatever your marital state right now, God intended it to bless you and not harm you. Walk daily in his good plan, and your future will be bright.

UNBIBLICAL VIEW #3: YOU ARE A REJECT AND NOT WORTHY OF ANYONE WHO WOULD TREAT YOU WELL

In this view, you tend to struggle with self-pity and self-rejection, focusing your anger on yourself. You feel as if God must have made a mistake when he made you. In this state of mind, you often allow abusive people to take advantage of you, which in a strange way seems to prove your suspicions about your unworthiness.

If you feel like a reject, I urge you to meditate on two stories from the Gospels. The first is the story of the leper who came to Jesus for healing. In this passage "a man with leprosy came to [Jesus] and begged him on his knees, 'If you are willing, you can make me clean.' Filled with compassion, Jesus reached out his hand and touched the man. 'I am willing,' he said. 'Be clean!' Immediately the leprosy left him and he was cured" (Mark 1:40–42). You may feel like a social leper. Maybe others treat you like one because of their own insecurities (though probably not as often as you imagine). But God never sees you like that.

Most people struggle relationally because they've never taken the time to let God show them who they are in Christ. They haven't yet discovered the unique gifts and abilities he has given them and to live with gusto without comparing themselves to others. True, there are some simple things we can and likely should change about ourselves if they are pointed out to us by loving friends—such as hygiene issues, irritating habits, unflattering hairstyles, etc. But the rest is God's handiwork, and he doesn't make junk.

The second passage is at the end of the parable of the prodigal son. It reminds us that our value is not determined by how we feel.

"So he got up and went to his father. But while he was still a long way off, his father saw him and was filled with compassion for him; he ran to his son, threw his arms around him and kissed him. The son said to him, 'Father, I have sinned against heaven and against you. I am no longer worthy to be called your son.' But the father said to his servants, 'Quick! Bring the best robe and put it on him. Put a ring on his finger and sandals on his feet. Bring the fattened calf and kill it. Let's have a feast and cele-brate. For this son of mine was dead and is alive again; he was lost and is found.' So they began to celebrate." (Luke 15:20–24)

How often I have heard words similar to what the prodigal son uttered above from the lips of someone trapped in a cycle of self-pity, self-rejection, and hopelessness: "I am not worthy." If you are there right now, you need to realize that the enemy has blinded you with lies. No matter your mistakes or sins, God stands ready to forgive you, cleanse you, and restore you as his child in the eyes of the world. All you have to do is confess, which means agree with God's opinion on the matter, and then repent, which means to start living 180 degrees in the other direction. Refusing to forgive yourself after God has forgiven and cleansed you is the equivalent of telling God he doesn't know what he is doing or that Jesus' death on the cross was not sufficient. Sane and stable people have but one alternative: to believe God over their feelings, forgive themselves, and get on with life.

Voluntary (and Temporary) Singleness

The issues discussed above apply primarily to people who are involuntarily single. Those self-esteem issues hit hardest when you desperately want to marry—or at least date—and you can't seem to make any progress in that direction. There are times, however, when it's a good idea not to date even when the opportunity presents itself. I'm not talking here about monks or nuns. I doubt they read many books about dating anyway. I'm talking about being voluntarily single for a season, and for a specific, temporary reason. Below are some good reasons not to date for a while.

1. You're taking a break to heal your heart or work on some of your personal baggage. This is very wise. When our hearts and perspectives are distorted by pain, confusion, and bad habits, we tend to make really bad decisions. One of the most common bad decisions made by those with baggage is serial dating. This entails dating people with similar dysfunctions and experiencing a destructive cycle of frustration. In other words, the names and faces of their dating partners change, but the relational and character dysfunctions remain the same. Doing this is like continually moving the same bad engine from car to car thinking a different model, color, or body style will somehow make the bad engine good. This relational blindness is caused by our attraction grid, which doesn't function correctly when the pain from our personal baggage skews our view of people—both positively and negatively. Taking a break can adjust our attraction grid by allowing necessary internal change and growth. When we are no longer blinded by pain, we can start making good relational decisions in dating.

2. You're simply not interested in the people you have met so far. That's fine. I would remind you, however, that Level One dating does not require attraction. Getting out there and having a little fun is healthy and may be

the doorway to meeting other more interesting folks you would not have met otherwise.

3. You're not dating because you feel called by God to remain single either for now or forever due to some personal mission.

I should say a couple of other things about this temporary, voluntary singleness. First, it's not an excuse to hide in your singleness in order to avoid the risk of rejection and failure due to past hurts. Second, even if you have good reasons for choosing to stay single—either temporarily or permanently—you need to be actively building a strong network of friendships in order to have the much-needed relational input and support of other people. This network acts as a relational support system, which is the subject of the next chapter.

CHAPTER FIVE

Your Relational Safety Net

Dating Lie #5: Your significant other can and should meet all your needs.

If you only get one thing out of this "interlude" on singleness, I want you to get this: God defines you. The people you date, the people who reject you, and even the person you eventually marry cannot give you true identity. God alone defines you.

Having said that, it's also important to recognize that every relationship in your life influences you either *toward* or *away* from what God has defined and designed you to be. This includes every relationship regardless of the context.

> The reality is that your dating relationships are only a part of a whole web of relationships.

Unfortunately, we tend to think that dating relationships are fundamentally different from other friendships. Some of this thinking rightly comes from the hope that one dating relationship will indeed develop into a relationship that is fundamentally different from all others—marriage. But it's important that you maintain a proper perspective on your dating relationships, especially at Levels One through Three.

The reality is that your dating relationships are only a part of a whole web of relationships. It's true that a dating relationship is likely to be more emotionally intense than most of your friendships, and you're liable to find yourself saying and doing things that you wouldn't in other friendships. But to maintain your Truth Triangle you must acknowledge this counterintuitive truth: until you get very deep into the Five Dating Levels, a dating relationship is not qualitatively different from your other friendships. I'm not saying that you shouldn't take dating seriously; I'm saying you should take all of your other relationships more seriously. The goal is to develop your entire web of relationships in such a way that you are relationally strong enough to date well.

> The Bible clearly teaches that, as image bearers of God, we are made for community.

The Bible clearly teaches that, as image bearers of God, we are made for community. The fact that babies who don't receive adequate touch and nurture can die[4] despite being fed seems to illustrate this truth. Human beings need relational interaction and support. We need to give and receive love. It is part of our developmental process and is crucial to our ongoing health and vitality. That kind of connection is one of the things people are looking for when they date, which is to be expected. But dating isn't the only way to build that connection, and it isn't even the most important way. What matters most is our larger web of relationships.

The Relational Safety Net

Whether you are single for life or married, to be healthy and happy you absolutely must have a sufficient and stable network of people who share life with you. Borrowing a concept from Dr. E. M. Pattison, this network of people acts as a psychosocial kinship system.[5] To better understand this idea, imagine that you were on the third floor of a burning building, and firefighters were standing below the window holding a safety net to break your fall. Hopefully there would be people on all four sides, and hopefully they would be strong enough (and sufficiently committed to their jobs) to catch you. In the same way, you need people in your everyday life who are there to catch you if you fall. Like the firefighters' net, this safety net works best when it is supported on all four sides. A healthy relational safety net therefore looks like this:

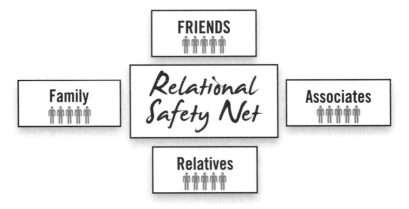

As you can see, it takes twenty to thirty people to support you, and it takes different kinds of relationships. Ideally, you should have five or six people in each group. If your family is sparse, far away, or too dysfunctional to be a part of your safety net, don't panic. Obviously, you can't choose your family. If that's your situation, you'll need to be more intentional about developing and maintaining friendships and associates that can take the place of family.

The main factors to consider in identifying those in your relational net are strength of the relationship and mutual commitment. These are people who would visit you if you were sick or would cross the street to say hello and not just smile and wave as you walked by. They are committed to being a part of your life far beyond that of a mere acquaintance. It's also important that these people come from the four categories of relationships mentioned above: immediate family, relatives, friends, and associates from work or church.

The people in your safety net don't just know you, they also know each other. When the members of your support team know each other, they naturally do a lot of the work to stay connected. That effort is naturally multiplied throughout the network when one member tries to connect with another through ordinary things like passing along a piece of news or a prayer request, or inviting a friend to have lunch. For example, among a network of friends, an invitation to play singles tennis can easily turn into a doubles match. By reaching out to one friend, you end up reconnecting with three.

The At-Risk Relational Safety Net

A person with less support will struggle with his or her relational health. A person who is at risk will have a relational net with only eight to twelve people and not many of those people will know each other. This is a fragmented community, and there are many holes through which this person's needs may

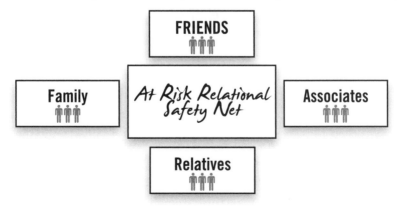

pass undetected or unmet. Because so few know each other, there is a much greater amount of stress and responsibility put on each individual to maintain their many relationships. Compare this with a healthy system, which allows a person to enjoy a much more restful existence because the community naturally stays connected.

The Dysfunctional Relational Network

An even more dangerous relational situation exists when a person has a relational net of only four to eight people. This situation is considered dysfunctional because 100 percent of the people know each other, but they are not necessarily in community. More likely, they are what some counselors call "enmeshed." They function as caretakers for a person who, for whatever reason, is no longer able to function well on his or her own.

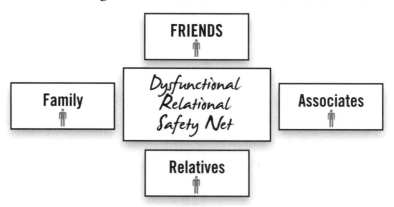

A dysfunctional relational safety net is a frazzled community due to the endless work required to deal with one person's dysfunction. Many of our elderly suffering from strokes or Alzheimer's disease experience this challenge, as do the families of the mentally ill and physically handicapped. People with social disorders, such as severe anxiety and obsessive-compulsive disorder, also tend to fall into this category.

Even for an otherwise healthy individual, staying in this relational condition is a recipe for disaster and often requires getting help from professionals to deal with the issues that led them to become so isolated. Those who are caretakers may need to press the issue in order to get such a person moving in the right direction.

What Causes an Unhealthy Relational Safety Net?

An unhealthy relational safety net isn't something that just happens. There are many factors that can hurt it, either temporarily or (if you're not proactive) permanently. The list below is in no way exhaustive, but it gives an idea of the range of things that can cause an unhealthy situation. Notice how common (and sometimes seemingly harmless) these causes can be.

1. A JOB LOSS OR TRANSFER

In our highly mobile society, no one seems to recognize the consequences of separation from family, childhood friends, and community relationships. The stress of moving to a new city and starting a new job can be overwhelming. Many fall into the trap of putting off finding a new community until they have more time. The problem is the free time they're waiting for never materializes. If we don't manage time, it manages us. The time crunch and the energy needed to walk into unfamiliar environments and meet new friends feels overwhelming to many and consequently never happens.

2. MOVING TO A NEW NEIGHBORHOOD

With traffic jams and sixty-hour workweeks, a simple move to a new neighborhood can put you far enough away from your relationships to have a dramatic effect. Combine this with new school districts and extracurricular events, and a few miles can seem like a universe away. The solution requires a lot of self-discipline and patience to rebuild what was lost. Talk to anyone who grew up in a military family and moved around a lot, and you'll get a feel for how disruptive this can be for some people.

3. THE DEATH OF A SPOUSE, DIVORCE, OR A BAD BREAKUP

When a spouse dies or leaves, a person's entire relational structure can be dramatically affected. This is especially true with a divorce. You can easily feel out of place in what used to be comfortable environments, and some people will not know how to relate with you in your new situation. Your emotional pain can also cause relational withdrawal, and you may find that your social skills are impaired, which can lead to more negative interactions than you are used to. The normal depression from grief can make meeting new people very difficult since you will rarely feel like yourself for many months.

4. UNDERDEVELOPED SOCIAL SKILLS

The next chapter will cover this in detail and contains an in-depth self-assessment test to determine what changes you might need to make in your own habits and attitudes to improve your relational skills.

5. CHANGING CHURCHES

As with moving to a new city, Christian singles often lose contact with 60 to 70 percent of their relational support when they change churches. While this is unavoidable when you change cities, the tendency to church hop in the same town can have severe and unintended consequences. Here again, we see the importance of learning how to date and end relationships well so that you don't alienate yourself from your church community.

What Can Be Done to Reverse the Damage to a Relational Safety Net?

If you find yourself in an at-risk condition, you must make a commitment to do simple things to change your situation. Get involved in a church, invite coworkers and/or neighbors to dinner or some fun event, join a club or organization that does things that interest you, or anything that enables you to make contact with new people who have the potential to become friends. If you don't have many (or any) family who can be a part of your support system, you must increase the number of friends you pursue and seek a few who can become as close as family. Eventually, with time and intentionality, you will once again find yourself part of a healthy relational network.

If you believe you are near or already in a dysfunctional condition, I urge you to contact a local Christian counselor to discuss ways of improving your situation. Nothing will change until you take that step. As hard as it may seem, a phone call can make all the difference in the world.

So, How Many People Are in Your Relational Safety Net?

Take a moment to write down your answers to the following questions:

1. How often do you talk with immediate family members?

   _____

   _____

   _____

   _____

2. How often do you talk with extended family/relatives?

   _____

   _____

_____

_____

3. How often do you talk with friends from church or the community?

_____

_____

_____

_____

4. How often do you talk with associates from work?

_____

_____

_____

_____

5. How many of your friends and family know each other?

_____

_____

_____

_____

6. When was the last time you spent time with each of these groups? What was the occasion?

_____

_____

_____

_____

7. What have you done recently to help or encourage the people who are a part of your safety net?

_____

_____

_____

_____

8. How comfortable are you in conversing with new people?

_____

_____

_____

_____

9. Recall the most recent extended conversation you have had with someone. How long did it last? What did you learn about them? Did they seem eager to end the conversation or to continue it?

_____

_____

_____

_____

10. Does the picture created by the sum of your answers sound similar to the healthy safety net or to one of the unhealthy ones? For instance, if you were unhappy with your answers to three or four questions, you are likely in an at-risk category. If you were unhappy with five to seven questions, you are likely in a dysfunctional category.

_____

_____

_____

_____

11. What changes do you feel like you need to make to improve the strength of your relationship safety net?

_____

_____

_____

_____

Conclusion

We tend to value rugged individualism in this country, but that's not a biblical view of who God made us to be. In his book, *Restoring Your Spiritual Passion*, Gordon MacDonald points out that the apostle Paul, as strong as he was, had a great need and a great capacity for friendship.[6] Paul was clearly committed to cultivating a band of special friends. He knew who they were, and he regularly recognized them for their contribution to his spiritual passion. His friends were a resource upon which he obviously depended and without which he would not have survived. A quick read through the New Testament shows us that Paul's friends Aquila, Priscilla, Onesiphorus, Philemon, Timothy, Luke, and many more were the people he lived out his life and faith with. They worked hard and shared food, tasks, joys, and sorrows. They encouraged each other and they suffered together. Paul's friends came from all ages and backgrounds, and he seems to have taken great care to grow and maintain his relationships.

> Joy, love, and purpose are what a healthy relational safety net will give you. God built us for community, which means relationships aren't just nice to have.

Think about Paul's network of relationships the next time you read a passage like Philippians 2:1–2: "If you have any encouragement from being united with Christ, if any comfort from his love, if any fellowship with the Spirit, if any tenderness and compassion, then make my joy complete by being like-minded, having the same love, being one in spirit and purpose." Joy, love, and purpose are what a healthy relational safety net will give you. God built us for community, which means relationships aren't just nice to have. You actually need relationships with friends, family, coworkers, and others. I know you're reading this book because you are interested specifically in dating relationships, But this is where healthy dating relationships start—with a healthy relational safety net.

As we have discussed, sometimes it is life situations that put a person's relational support system at risk. But sometimes

> Healthy dating relationships start with a healthy relational safety net.

the issues are internal. Strengthening your relational safety net isn't always a matter of changing your circumstances. Often it requires changing yourself. The good news is that you can change.

CHAPTER SIX

Is There Something Wrong with Me?

Dating Lie #6: I must be a loser because I'm not in a relationship.

When people are single, they often ask the question, "Is there something wrong with me?" Of course there's something wrong with you. There's something wrong with everybody. We're all sinners, and we all have issues. Being single is not a punishment for being an imperfect human being. Keep in mind however that your specific issues and hang-ups may make it difficult for you to have healthy relationships, including dating relationships. It's very likely that you (like everybody else) could benefit from some serious self-assessment, which can be painful. Believe me, I know firsthand that an unexamined life guarantees an undeveloped soul, unnecessary suffering, and unexplainable relational frustration. If you want healthy relationships, you have to start with the person in the mirror.

> It's very likely that you (like everybody else) could benefit from some serious self-assessment, which can be painful.

This chapter is all about taking a good look in the mirror so that you can do two things: (1) honestly face any negative issues in

50

your life that you *can* change with God's help, and (2) resolve once and for all that you will only let God define you.

Each of us has room to grow and develop. Even Jesus when he came to earth went through the human process of growth spiritually, mentally, emotionally, physically, and socially. "Jesus grew in wisdom and stature, and in favor with God and men" (Luke 2:52). That's pretty remarkable when you think about it. Jesus was God

> If you want healthy relationships, you have to start with the person in the mirror.

made flesh, and yet he grew and changed. He built relationships and, in doing so, increased in favor with God as well as the people around him. Why, then, should we feel ashamed to admit that we need to grow and to change mentally, emotionally, physically, spiritually, and socially?

The fact that you need to grow isn't evidence that you're a loser (unless, of course, you choose not to grow). Your growth is part of God's plan. Consider what Paul wrote to the Thessalonians: "*May God himself, the God of peace, sanctify you through and through.* May your whole spirit, soul and body be kept blameless at the coming of our Lord Jesus Christ. The one who calls you is faithful and *he will do it*" (1 Thessalonians 5:23-24, emphasis added). *Sanctify* is just the theological word for changing into the person God would have you to be. And as this verse shows, not only is your sanctification part of God's plan, he is faithful to carry out his plan in your life. 2 Corinthians 3:18 says it beautifully: "And we, who with unveiled faces all reflect the Lord's glory, are being transformed into his likeness with ever-increasing glory, which comes from the Lord, who is the Spirit."

God carries out his plan, but you have to be intentional too. The world has a way of conforming you to itself when you take the path of least resistance. That's why you have to "be transformed by the renewing of your mind" (Romans 12:2). If you truly want to change and grow, you've got to get a new way of thinking. It's not enough to hear or read the truth and nod your head in agreement. Nodding your head isn't going to get you where you want to be. "Do not merely listen to the word, and so deceive yourselves. Do what it says. Anyone who listens to the word but does not do what it says is like a man who looks at his face in a mirror and, after looking at himself, goes away and immediately forgets what he looks like. But the man who looks intently into the perfect law that gives freedom, and continues to do this, not forgetting what he has heard, but doing it—he will be blessed in what he does" (James 1:22–25). James's direct words force us to ask, "Am I willing to let the Spirit of God show me the things he wants me to focus on?"

A Look in the Mirror

You've probably seen one of the makeover reality shows where an ugly duckling is transformed into a beautiful swan right before your eyes. At the beginning of the hour, she's sitting in front of a mirror seeing the same old self she's seen every day of her life. Then the makeover consultant comes and says, "Look what we can do with those cheekbones. Here's how we can highlight your eyes. Are you sure a person your age should have bangs?" Suddenly the woman in the chair sees in the mirror something she has never seen before, and everything is different.

Perhaps the hardest thing about looking in the mirror is knowing whether or not you see what you're supposed to see. We all have major blind spots when it comes to our own lives. Actually, I would suggest that we can't see what we really need to see—not on our own anyway. The good news is that the Holy Spirit is always willing to show us exactly where we need to change. As Jesus promised, "The Counselor, the Holy

Spirit, whom the Father will send in my name, will teach you all things and will remind you of everything I have said to you" (John 14:26). That's good news that offers real comfort. As you look into the mirror of Scripture, you have a personal spiritual makeover consultant right there at your shoulder.

> We can't see what we really need to see—not on our own anyway. The good news is that the Holy Spirit is always willing to show us exactly where we need to change.

Below you'll find a three-step process that consists of praying, reading and meditating on Scripture, and self-assessment. These steps will help you take a look in the mirror in a good and healthy way. To get you started I've provided some specific Scripture verses to help with the reading and meditating. Following the Scripture, you'll find a brief self-assessment tool that will help you locate where you are personally and relationally by giving you concrete ideas of where change is needed.

STEP 1: PRAY

Don't skip this all-important first step in your eagerness to get to the Scriptures and the self-assessment. Stop and pray, asking the Holy Spirit to reveal whatever he wants to reveal to you.

STEP 2: READ AND MEDITATE

Read and meditate on the following verses and take note of anything the Spirit seems to bring to the surface.

Matthew 22:36–40 (Relationship with God)

"Teacher, which is the greatest commandment in the Law?" Jesus replied: "'Love the Lord your God with all your heart and with all your soul and with all your mind.' This is the first and greatest commandment. And the second is like it: 'Love your neighbor as yourself.' All the Law and the Prophets hang on these two commandments."

Personal Notes:

_____

_____

_____

_____

_____

_____

_____

Perhaps no one has ever explained to you how to have a relationship with God. It would be an honor for me to do so right now! The Bible says that all of us have been born with a terminal disease called sin...it is spiritual cancer. There is no hope for us unless God is allowed to apply spiritual radiation—the blood of Jesus Christ and the indwelling power of the Holy Spirit—to this sin-cancer. Only the price paid by Jesus on the cross with his blood can pay our sin-debt, and only the spiritual chemotherapy of the Holy Spirit living inside of us can break the power of sin in our lives. The result is that we are set free from the penalty of sin and from the power of sin, which is why we call it the good news! If you want this and are willing to let God come inside to forgive you, cleanse you, heal you, and take control of your life, then pray the following prayer and he will do all of these things:

> *Lord, I'm a sinner and can't heal myself. I thank you for sending Jesus to die in my place and pay my sin-debt. Jesus, I receive you now as my Savior and Lord and ask you to come live inside of me by your Holy Spirit. Forgive me, cleanse me, heal me, and take control. Teach me how to cooperate with you and begin to transform me from the inside out. Thank you, Lord, in Jesus' name, Amen!*

Jeremiah 29:11 (Life Focus)

"For I know the plans I have for you," declares the LORD, "plans to prosper you and not to harm you, plans to give you hope and a future."

Personal Notes:

_____

_____

_____

_____

_____

_____

Colossians 3:12–14 (Relational Safety Net)

"Therefore, as God's chosen people, holy and dearly loved, clothe yourselves with compassion, kindness, humility, gentleness and patience. Bear with each other and forgive whatever grievances you may have against one another. Forgive as the Lord forgave you. And over all these virtues put on love, which binds them all together in perfect unity."

Personal Notes:

_____

_____

_____

_____

_____

_____

Philippians 4:4–9 (Emotional State)

"Rejoice in the Lord always. I will say it again: Rejoice! Let your gentleness be evident to all. The Lord is near. Do not be anxious about anything, but in everything, by prayer and petition, with thanksgiving, present your requests to God. And the peace of God, which transcends all understanding, will guard your hearts and your minds in Christ Jesus.

"Finally, brothers, whatever is true, whatever is noble, whatever is right, whatever is pure, whatever is lovely, whatever is admirable—if anything is excellent or praiseworthy—think about such things. Whatever you have learned or received or heard from me, or seen in me—put it into practice. And the God of peace will be with you."

Personal Notes:

_____

_____

_____

_____

_____

_____

Ephesians 4:29–32: (Communication Skills)

"Do not let any unwholesome talk come out of your mouths, but only what is helpful for building others up according to their needs, that it may benefit those who listen. And do not grieve the Holy Spirit of God, with whom you were sealed for the day of redemption. Get rid of all bitterness, rage and anger, brawling and slander, along with every form of malice. Be kind and compassionate to one another, forgiving each other, just as in Christ God forgave you."

Personal Notes:

_____

_____

_____

_____

_____

_____

Ephesians 5:15–16: (Time Management)

"Be very careful, then, how you live—not as unwise but as wise, making the most of every opportunity, because the days are evil."

Personal Notes:

_____

_____

_____

_____

_____

_____

Proverbs 10:2–5 (Money Management)

"Ill-gotten treasures are of no value, but righteousness delivers from death. The LORD does not let the righteous go hungry but he thwarts the craving of the wicked. Lazy hands make a man poor, but diligent hands bring wealth. He who gathers crops in summer is a wise son, but he who sleeps during harvest is a disgraceful son."

Personal Notes:

_____

_____

_____

_____

_____

_____

STEP 3: SELF-ASSESSMENT

Take a minute to assess yourself using the scale below.

Assessment Scale

Rate yourself from 1 to 10 on each of the seven issues below using the descriptive phrases to determine where you are on the scale. You should focus on improving areas where you scored a 5 or below.

Relationship with God

1 .... **5** **10**

No Personal Faith	Consistent Devotions	Deep Faith
	Biblical Value System	Biblical Lifestyle
	Committed to Growth	Equipping Others
	Committed to Community	Faithful Service

Life Focus

1 .... **5** **10**

Drifting	Focused and Self-starting	Flourishing Career
No Direction	Living on Your Own	Mentoring Others
	Clarifying Long-term Goals	Mastering Skills

Relational Safety Net

1 .... **5** **10**

No Friendships	Several Acquaintances	Many Acquaintances
Codependent	Some Casual Friends	Several Casual Friends
Family Issues Unresolved	Adequate Close Friends	Abundant Close Friends
	Healing Family Issues	Stable Family
	Clarifying Boundaries	Clear Boundaries

Emotional State

1	5	10
Anger and Bitterness	Healing Anger and Bitterness	Free from Past Hurts
Unhealthy Relationships	Clarifying Attraction Grid	Healthy and Biblical Grid
Negative Attitude	Generally Positive	Upbeat and Hopeful
Dysfunctional Patterns	Unlearning Bad Patterns	Healthy Patterns Established

Communication Skills

1	5	10
Deception	Aware and Honest about Feelings	Vulnerable and Transparent
Weak Conversation Skills	Learning Conversation Skills	Good Conversation Skills
Frequent Conflict	Open and Approachable	Speaks Truth in Love

Time Management

1	5	10
Unmanaged Life	Establishing Time Boundaries	Balance Maintained
Chaos and Unhealthy Priorities	Clarifying Priorities	Productive and Paced
Unreliable	Learning Time Management Skills	Skills Mastered

Money Management

1	5	10
No Budget	Budget Established	Staying on Budget
Consistently in Debt	Debt Being Reduced	Debt Free
No Savings	$1000 Emergency Fund	3-6 Month Reserve and Investing
No Giving	Tithing Practiced	Tithing and Sacrificial Giving

Now that you have an idea of what God might want you to work on, make an appointment with a pastor, personal coach, counselor, or mentor to talk through some specific ways to create a personal growth plan. Make sure the plan includes some specifics for how to move forward.

Who Defines You?

All this soul-searching and self-assessment can be a little depressing. When we look in the mirror, we don't always like what we see. But be encouraged by remembering how we started this chapter: God defines you. A self-assessment might describe where you are, and your inner critic might display what you're afraid of becoming. But only God can truly define who you are.

Basically, you have two options: God defines you or people do. Those people may include yourself, a parent, a spouse, a friend, an old teacher, or even a pastor. Many of those human beings are benevolent toward you and have the best intentions. Even so, I assure you that the absolute best thing for any person is for God to define him or her. Human judges, mentors, and critics are imperfect even in their finest moments. They cannot clearly or completely see your future or your soul. Only God can do that.[7] Read and meditate on the following verses to better understand this truth and many other truths that are yours in Christ. Write down anything that encourages you beneath each passage.

God created you with a plan in mind

"For we are God's workmanship, created in Christ Jesus to do good works, which God prepared in advance for us to do" (Ephesians 2:10).

Personal Notes:

_____

_____

_____

_____

_____

_____

You are wonderfully made

"For you created my inmost being; you knit me together in my mother's womb. I praise you because I am fearfully and wonderfully made; your works are wonderful, I know that full well. My frame was not hidden from you when I was made in the secret place. When I was woven together in the depths of the earth, your eyes saw my unformed body. All the days ordained for me were written in your book before one of them came to be" (Psalm 139:13–16).

Personal Notes:

_____

_____

_____

_____

_____

_____

You are God's child

"How great is the love the Father has lavished on us, that we should be called children of God! And that is what we are! The reason the world does not know us is that it did not know him. Dear friends, now we are children of God, and what we will be has not yet been made known. But we know that when he appears, we shall be like him, for we shall see him as he is. Everyone who has this hope in him purifies himself, just as he is pure" (1 John 3:1–3).

Personal Notes:

_____

_____

_____

_____

_____

_____

You are God's friend

"Greater love has no one than this, that he lay down his life for his friends. You are my friends if you do what I command. I no longer call you servants, because a servant does not know his master's business. Instead, I have called you friends, for everything that I learned from my Father I have made known to you" (John 15:13–15).

Personal Notes:

_____

_____

_____

_____

_____

_____

You are accepted by God and are not condemned

"Accept one another, then, just as Christ accepted you, in order to bring praise to God" (Romans 15:7).

Personal Notes:

_____

_____

_____

_____

_____

_____

You need not fear condemnation

"Therefore, there is now no condemnation for those who are in Christ Jesus, because through Christ Jesus the law of the Spirit of life set me free from the law of sin and death" (Romans 8:1–2).

Personal Notes:

_____

_____

_____

_____

_____

_____

You have been chosen by God to have a fruitful life

"You did not choose me, but I chose you and appointed you to go and bear fruit—fruit that will last. Then the Father will give you whatever you ask in my name" (John 15:16).

Personal Notes:

_____

_____

_____

_____
_____
_____

You have been made full and complete in Christ

"So then, just as you received Christ Jesus as Lord, continue to live in him, rooted and built up in him, strengthened in the faith as you were taught, and overflowing with thankfulness. See to it that no one takes you captive through hollow and deceptive philosophy, which depends on human tradition and the basic principles of this world rather than on Christ. For in Christ all the fullness of the Deity lives in bodily form, and you have been given fullness in Christ, who is the head over every power and authority" (Colossians 2:6–10).

Personal Notes:

_____
_____
_____
_____
_____
_____

You can do all things through Christ

"I am not saying this because I am in need, for I have learned to be content whatever the circumstances. I know what it is to be in need, and I know what it is to have plenty. I have learned the secret of being content in any and every situation, whether well fed or hungry, whether living in plenty or in want. I can do everything through him who gives me strength" (Philippians 4:11–13).

Personal Notes:

You can participate in the divine nature

"His divine power has given us everything we need for life and godliness through our knowledge of him who called us by his own glory and goodness. Through these he has given us his very great and precious promises, so that through them you may participate in the divine nature and escape the corruption in the world caused by evil desires" (2 Peter 1:3–4).

Personal Notes:

Nothing can separate you from God's love

"And we know that in all things God works for the good of those who love him, who have been called according to his purpose. For those God foreknew he also predestined to be conformed to the likeness of his Son, that he might be the firstborn among many brothers. And those he predestined, he also called; those he called, he also justified; those he justified, he also glorified.

"What, then, shall we say in response to this? If God is for us, who can be against us? He who did not spare his own Son, but gave him up for us all—how will he not also, along with him, graciously give us all things? Who will bring any charge against those whom God has chosen? It is God who justifies. Who is he that condemns? Christ Jesus, who died—more than that, who was raised to life—is at the right hand of God and is also interceding for us. Who shall separate us from the love of Christ? Shall trouble or hardship or persecution or famine or nakedness or danger or sword? As it is written:

'For your sake we face death all day long;
we are considered as sheep to be slaughtered.'

No, in all these things we are more than conquerors through him who loved us. For I am convinced that neither death nor life, neither angels nor demons, neither the present nor the future, nor any powers, neither height nor depth, nor anything else in all creation, will be able to separate us from the love of God that is in Christ Jesus our Lord" (Romans 8:28–39).

Personal Notes:

_____
_____
_____
_____
_____
_____

God created you. You're his child and his friend. You're accepted by him, you've been chosen by him, you've been made complete in him, and you can do all things through him. Why wouldn't you want to believe him over anything anyone else says!

Dating for Something to Do

Because we live in a mobile society, many singles live in cities far from home. This means that dating is a lot harder than it was a generation ago. Think about it—if you don't meet your future spouse in college, once you follow career opportunities to a new city, the pond you're fishing in gets very small, very fast. You don't know anybody, and there is no clear and safe social network to join. On top of that, you're probably working fifty to sixty hours a week, which exponentially increases the difficulty of finding a substantial group of friends, much less potential dates. Your well-meaning mother calls and innocently asks, "Have you met anybody special?" "Anybody special?" you want to scream, "I haven't even met my next-door neighbor!"

Well-developed friendship networks enable people to get to know one another enough to determine if an actual date is warranted. Without this network, healthy casual social contact with other singles becomes significantly more difficult and increases the pressure people feel to make a connection. Without the casual socializing, how do you know whether you're making a good decision to ask somebody out? How do you keep your intentions and interest level from being misunderstood? For that matter, how can you understand your own intentions and interest level without a first date?

I remember a man telling me he was about ready to give up dating and become a monk. He shared his frustration at trying to date without feeling obligated to continue dating if things went badly or simply fell flat. I marveled as I realized that this sharp, good-looking, intelligent, stable, and godly man with a great sense of humor hadn't been on a date in a long time. Even more amazing was that I knew there were many single women in our church who would have loved to go out with him. He had been holding back because of several past experiences in which women (and their friends) misinterpreted one or two dates as interest in a long-term relationship. When he decided he did not want to continue dating, the relationship would get awkward, and in some cases, he would receive negative responses from the woman and her circle of friends. "How can I know if a woman is someone I'd want to spend the rest of my life with unless I spend lots of time with her," he asked. "But when I spend time with women to see if we are well suited, it gets confusing. And if we don't seem well suited, feelings get hurt, and I lose not only a dating relationship, but someone with whom I could have been good friends."

Like so many single men and women I talk to, this man found himself in a classic chicken-and-egg predicament. Too often this results in less dating, or no dating. When people live in fear of failure, they stagnate. The first step to breaking out of this "analysis paralysis" is to redefine what we mean by a "date" and then adjust our expectations. I am convinced that more men would ask women out on more dates more often if everyone understood and accepted the perspective of a Level One date: no obligation for the future. I am equally convinced that with this same perspective, more women would accept invitations to go out on simple, fun dates, resulting in less rejection for men. More dates, less rejection. What single adult would be opposed to that?

By the way, the man who was thinking about becoming a monk never went through with it. Now he's a husband and a father, and it all began with Level One dating.

CHAPTER SEVEN

What Is Level One Dating?

Dating Lie #7: There are no rules in dating; it's all about romance.

When I first started teaching singles about the Five Dating Levels, their initial reaction was that it sounded too rigid and unromantic. But once they tried it, they discovered the boundaries offered more freedom because they created a safe space where they could be themselves. Believe me, having to make things up as you go along is not freedom. For example, when there is a fence around a playground, kids are more relaxed, they play more, and they explore more. When there is no fence, they have a tendency to huddle in the middle of the playground, or worse, run out into traffic! Boundaries provide clear parameters in which to play and offer protection to all.

The Five Dating Levels help define where a couple is every step of the way in terms of their commitments and expectations, so that they can relax and enjoy the journey. Because boundaries are clear a couple can easily get on the same page and find plenty of room for spontaneity and romance. Just as importantly, they find it easier and safer to stop dating without hurting each other.

Of all the levels, Level One is the simplest and surprisingly most often overlooked. It involves simple activity-centered events that can be a onetime date or one of many dates where you get to know someone. If this sounds overly casual, good; it's supposed to! Calling this level "Dating for Something to Do" highlights that this is nothing serious and shouldn't be taken too seriously—not yet anyway. Not taking these dates too seriously doesn't mean treating the person you're dating dismissively or with little respect. You should take seriously your responsibility to respect the boundaries of a Level One date and keep your Truth Triangle in balance. But you should *not* treat the date as the first step on the road to marriage. It probably isn't.

What a Level One Date Might Look Like

In the introduction I used visiting the mall as a metaphor for a dating relationship. Let's return to the mall to talk about what Level One dating looks like.

Prior to dating anyone, you go to the mall by yourself or maybe with a group of friends. While there you are very aware of the people around you—especially certain members of the opposite sex. You have fun, talk with your friends, and shop. You may enjoy a meal or a movie, or you may just sit and watch the world go by. All in all it is simple fun without pressure or confusion. But if you are on a Level One date a visit to the mall will have some important differences that might look like the following paragraphs.

You might start by meeting the person with whom you are going on a Level One date at the mall. You could ride together, but for the first date, the safety of having your own ride home reduces the sense of risk. You and your date are meeting a group of friends at the mall because group settings make it easier to keep emotions in check, and it also makes things more tolerable if the date is going poorly.

Because you both have clarified your intentions, the atmosphere is light and carefree. You have agreed that this is simply an event for fun. You will each pay your own way to avoid any kind of misunderstanding or sense of obligation. You have made no obligation to go out again so you can relax and be yourself. If either of you does not desire to go out with the other in the future, there should be no ill will. You simply enjoyed a day of fun together and you will leave it at that. In fact, you can enjoy this type of date with multiple people if you so desire.

Level One is the simplest and surprisingly most often overlooked. It involves simple activity-centered events that can be a onetime date or one of many dates where you get to know someone.

With your bearings clearly understood, you casually stroll along, seeing what comes your way, enjoying the activity. You talk about the things you see, and the people you pass. Together you enter stores that appeal to one or the other, or both. This enables you to learn about each other. The conversation skims along the surface; it's interesting, it reveals a little bit, but it's still pretty safe—nothing too personal at this level.

You go into the Apple Store to check out their latest computer or see what's playing at the movie theater. You learn about what the other likes to do for fun, as well as getting a taste of his or her value system regarding cultural standards and beliefs. Next, you wander into the Hallmark store to get a birthday card for your mom. This provides an opportunity to talk a little about your families. Again, you're not sharing too much, but enough to gain a basic understanding of who this person is.

As you walk and talk you might be attracted to your date. If it happens, the attraction will begin by really noticing the person. This is called eye-to-body contact. It is a moment of discovery! It is not sexual in nature, but a strong realization that the person is in the room. If this moment of connection doesn't happen, that's okay too. After all, this is casual.

My Story: The Moment of Discovery

I will never forget when I had this moment of discovery with my wife, Kim. It is burned into my memory like a living snapshot. Though I had known her for years and thought she was pretty, I had never really seen her before as I did in that moment. I was preaching my first sermon to a large group of singles, and Kim was in the crowd. My eyes scanned across the room while I was explaining a point in my talk, and I saw her! Literally, it felt like time stood still and my eyes had a telescopic lens. I zoomed in on her face. She was smiling, seemingly encouraging me from her seat. Her new haircut accentuated her beautiful face...and those eyes. To this day, I can conjure up that image and feel the emotions and excitement I felt in that moment.

A lot of the mystery of attraction is at work here, and we may never completely understand how it works. While not all aspects of our attraction mechanism are healthy (due to past wounds and the effects of sin), many of them are good, and they all have a powerful effect on us. If your date does not notice you at the same time, there will typically be hours, days, or even weeks of hoping they will return and hold the glance of possibility. It's highly possible that they won't ever return that glance. Remember, we're still at Level One, and keeping a balanced Truth Triangle requires that you free both yourself and your date from expectations.

That first moment of attraction can truly be powerful, but it is only the beginning. If the attraction is strong enough and you continue your stroll through the mall, you may also experience the eye-to-eye game of visual tag. Let's say that the group decides to go into the mall restaurant for dinner. If both you and your date notice each other simultaneously, there will be a series of brief eye contacts that cause the heart to race and the face to flush. It is an almost embarrassing sensation, as if someone has seen into your unguarded heart. As you sit around the table, your eyes bouncing back and forth, you may feel the urge to hold the other person's hand or make some other minor physical contact. This is an urge you need to resist. Any such contact in Level One will disrupt the development process and confuse everyone involved. So you take a big sip of cold water and focus your attention on voice-to-voice interaction. The pattern you set for talking and sharing at this point is very important for any future interaction.

So you begin the stressful process of actually talking to each other. Trying to figure out what to say and how to begin a conversation consumes your attention. The point at this stage is mostly the sheer joy of hearing the other's voice and being in contact. As you eat your food and share conversation and laughs with the group at the table, you are especially attuned to the sound of one particular voice.

By the way, sometimes eye-to-body and eye-to-eye contact can happen quickly and before you've been officially introduced. This can cause a great deal of stress as you try to figure out how to meet and have voice-to-voice contact. Most cultures develop formal and acceptable ways of approaching a member of the opposite sex to assist with this awkward stage. Matchmakers, mutual friends, speed dating events, and even the tired old library of pick-up lines are considered in this process.

Although I've been emphasizing the casual nature of this Level One date, I don't wish to suggest that what is happening here is unimportant. To underestimate the power of the bonding interaction in this first dating level is a huge mistake. It forms the basis for keeping the heart stirred later on, and though you move to other levels beyond eye-to-body, eye-to-eye, and voice-to-voice, you will never stop repeating the process—even with your future spouse after you get married.

Two Tests of Character at Level One

As you leave the restaurant the group says their goodbyes and begins to disperse. If there has been no attraction, you politely say goodbye and go home. However, if you experienced the attraction and bonding interaction described above, you face two real tests of your character.

TEST 1: MAINTAINING THE BOUNDARIES OF YOUR LEVEL OF COMMITMENT

Remember, you agreed that the date was simply a fun time with friends at the mall. Now that everyone is leaving, despite the attraction, you must bring the date to an end. For example, going out alone for coffee and dessert afterward may create the wrong impression and put too much pressure on willpower weakened by a few hours of strong attraction. If you both desire to spend more time together, go out again in the future. The excitement of waiting is good for the relational development process. When the activity is over, go home!

TEST 2: MAINTAINING YOUR TRUTH TRIANGLE

As you will remember, the Truth Triangle is about staying balanced as you navigate through the Dating Levels. One of the main reasons people have problems in their dating relationships is because their *behaviors* don't match what they have been allowing themselves to *think and feel.*

If you find yourself attracted to the other person during the event and disappointed that they don't seem to reciprocate the attraction, commit yourself to praying for God to bless that person's life and for him to guide you to other people to spend time with. God does answer prayer, and you can't be mad or sulk if you are praying.

Let's use the mall example to demonstrate what it might look like when a Truth Triangle gets out of balance. You are at the mall on a Level One date. The attraction is strong, and the eye contact and conversation are really connecting. As you sit there with the group (we'll pretend you're the woman for the purposes of this example), you begin to think to yourself how your first name would sound with his last name. You are daydreaming about your date and a more committed relationship. He is feeling the attraction as well and begins to hold your hand under the table. Both of you are making serious (though common) mistakes.

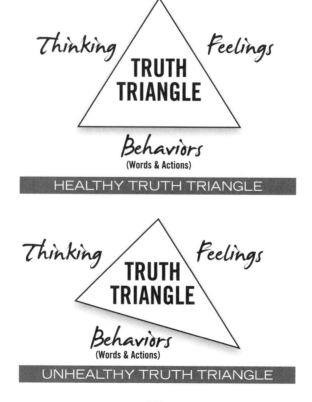

Thinking   Feelings

TRUTH TRIANGLE

Behaviors
(Words & Actions)

HEALTHY TRUTH TRIANGLE

Thinking   Feelings

TRUTH TRIANGLE

Behaviors
(Words & Actions)

UNHEALTHY TRUTH TRIANGLE

First, you are not exercising self-control over your emotions or thinking.

While your emotions are strong and real, they are not based on reality at this point, but on a perception of possibility. To act upon them as if they were time tested and accurate would be foolish. You can will your mind to think within healthy boundaries, which makes it easier to rein in your emotions and get them under control. Emotions fluctuate rapidly and come and go with time. A mature person recognizes this and doesn't allow emotions to distort his or her view of reality, refusing either to be deceived or be a deceiver.

> Emotions fluctuate rapidly and come and go with time. A mature person recognizes this and doesn't allow emotions to distort his or her view of reality, refusing either to be deceived or be a deceiver.

Second, he is not exercising self-control over his behaviors.

By leaping to physical interaction that is reserved for a later bonding stage, he is creating a false sense of commitment. The next day, after the magic of the moment has passed, it is very likely that he will struggle with regret for implying more commitment than he is willing to make at this point.

What if you've already blown it?

Perhaps you are in a relationship right now and you have already moved too far and too fast, either emotionally or physically. You can repair the damage to the relationship. This will require being humble enough to go to the other person and honestly admit your mistake and ask for forgiveness. By explaining that you were caught up in the moment and later realized that you didn't protect the other person or yourself from false expectations, you have the chance to back up and put the relationship back on solid and honest footing. At the very least the other person can be encouraged that you actually did experience the emotions of the moment with them—which is saying something. All that is needed is time and a healthy process to test the reality of that moment for the long haul. Done well, this can actually strengthen a relationship that may have potential. Not doing this will plant a time bomb in your relationship that will go off unexpectedly in the future.

Hopefully, the importance of the Truth Triangle is becoming apparent. By conscientiously working to keep your thoughts, feelings, and behaviors in alignment, you are able to move as slowly as you need to in order to give the bonding process time to fully work at each level. This will also help you decide when to move forward and go to the next dating level. You will be able to trust yourself because you will know that you have allowed time and process to test your perceptions and the potential of the relationship. You can be confident that you are not being deceived by your emotions.

Touchstones at Level One

Each level of dating brings certain character tests into play. Here are some of the biggest tests at Level One:

- *Stick with the time boundary. Don't linger after the activity has ended. Otherwise, you can very easily find yourself swept up in a magic moment that will create a false sense of commitment. There will be plenty of time for magic moments later in the journey.*
- *Keep your Truth Triangle balanced. If attraction happens, it is critical to avoid moving too fast.*
- *Maintain appropriate personal space. For example, riding together at this level (especially the first time) is an unnecessary risk. Also,*

allowing one person to pay for everything creates a sense of obligation that should not be allowed at Level One. And finally, not being with a group or in a very public place tends to put too much pressure on the relationship, especially for the first couple of dates.

Some of you reading this might be thinking, "That just sounds too restrictive, I don't need to listen to these suggestions. I'm an adult. I can handle myself." I can't tell you how many times I have sat with a person or a couple in a counseling situation and listened to them recount the pain and suffering they have endured because they thought they were the exception to the rule. You are not the exception to the rule. You are a normal human being just like everyone else. I plead with you to trust me on this. If you follow the plan, you won't regret it!

CHAPTER EIGHT

Communication at Level One

Dating Lie #8: Just dive-in; it's better to discuss expectations later.

Remember the story of the Tower of Babel? At one time, everyone in the world spoke a common language. But when the people set out to build a tower to heaven to assert their autonomy, God confused their language. This made it much harder for them to get anything done, let alone build an enormous tower.

Basic communication has been confusing and difficult since the day Babel earned its name. Dating is one of those areas where that truth is most evident. Sure, we may both be speaking English, but sometimes it sounds like a foreign language. Singles need a common language that would allow them to be specific, clear, and honest about dating. The Five Dating Levels provides the structure to support good communication.

Communication is an incredible gift and privilege God has given to us. Yet, when we abuse this privilege by not communicating with each other or doing so in a hurtful or deceitful way, we sow seeds of mistrust, confusion, and pain. Like everything

> Communication is an incredible gift and privilege God has given to us.

else in life, if you use communication to understand God's will and nourish the person you are dating, God will bless your relationship. Ignore or abuse communication, and God will frustrate your plans. It is one of the many ways he protects us from hurting others, deceiving ourselves, and missing out on the good things he wants to give us.

I cannot emphasize enough the importance of good communication in dating relationships, which includes before they begin and even after they're over. When you combine temperament issues and gender differences with the simple reality of our sinful natures, it is a wonder men and women talk to each other at all. But we do and we must if we are going to experience the wonderful gift of relationship God has given to mankind—the ability to emotionally and relationally connect with one another! When applied to dating, the first thing you need to understand about communication is how to get started.

Starting from the Same Place

You've probably beat me to the punch on the next question. In a world where the prevailing ideas about dating are very different from the principles of the Five Dating Levels, how do you get on the same page with someone *before* you begin dating? How do you explain the Dating Levels so that you both start at Level One? You may have already imagined an awkward conversation that begins with you saying, "So, there's this thing called the Five Dating Levels…" How do you accomplish this in a way that feels normal and natural, especially when the other person has never heard of these concepts?

First, let me state that it's probably okay to ask someone on a Level One date without getting into the whole explanation of the Dating Levels. Sometimes the situations in which you see the person would not allow such a conversation. If that's the case, be prepared to have the conversation either during the event or at another time over coffee or lunch if you decide you want to spend more time with that person. I strongly recommend that if you don't talk about it on the first date, you plan the second date in such a way as to allow for this conversation. This will prevent the relationship from falling into the same old worldly rut, which will produce the same old negative results. Remember, the purpose of the Dating Levels is to protect one another from misunderstandings and provide a common framework for clear discussion along the way.

> Remember, the purpose of the Dating Levels is to protect one another from misunderstandings and provide a common framework for clear discussion along the way.

HOW TO INTRODUCE THE FIVE DATING LEVELS: A STEP-BY-STEP GUIDE

When it's time to have a conversation about the Dating Levels, consider the following ideas:

1. Pick a location where it is quiet enough to talk but wouldn't typically be thought of as a romantic place.
2. Choose a safe activity such as coffee or lunch.
3. Enjoy simple small talk for a little while and then start the conversation with something like the following:

> You seem like a lot of fun! I enjoy doing things with lots of different people and would like to go to

a concert or movie with you sometime. But if we do, I'd like to talk with you about something first. I believe men and women can take a lot of the hassles and confusion out of dating if they follow some simple principles I read about in a great book on healthy relationships. It lays out some basic guidelines to follow for setting expectations in order to avoid misunderstandings and hurt feelings. It allows you to relax and enjoy the journey—whether the journey ends after a couple of dates or develops into something more. I'd like to show you these guidelines and see what you think. Would you be okay with that?

I know that right now reading this you may be thinking, "I could never do that!" I know it seems awkward, and maybe a little uncomfortable to have this kind of conversation this early in a dating relationship. But it's not nearly as awkward or uncomfortable as the miscommunication, the hurt feelings, and the other sticky situations that inevitably arise when two people have different expectations for a relationship.

Perhaps you would say, "It seems so mechanical, where is the mystery and romance?" My answer to you is that there will be plenty of opportunity for mystery and romance, but only if the relationship moves beyond one or two fun activities. Why would you want to let your emotions get upside down over a person you don't even really know yet? That attitude is not only relationally immature but biblically unwise.

Or maybe you would say, "It seems so forward. What if they aren't interested and say no?" If they aren't interested in exploring a better way to date, do you really want to date them and go down the same old path yet again? If they are intimidated by such a simple and honest conversation now, what makes you think they would be willing to talk about such things later on in the relationship? At least you found out sooner rather than later. Or what if they willingly discuss the material but decline your invitation to do something fun? Again, be glad that you found out sooner rather than later. Whether they aren't attracted to you or they want to date without clear boundaries, either way you're better off knowing now and moving on, right?

I am fairly confident that the vast majority of people will be willing to read the material and talk about it, and many will embrace it with relief. I have shared this with literally hundreds of singles and have always gotten a great response and lots of follow-up questions as they began to put it into action.

4. If the other person agrees to talk about the Dating Levels, use the quick summary below as a reference tool. You might also go back to the introduction section of this book to review the details. It will be best if you spend time familiarizing yourself with the details of the chart so that you can explain it in your own words, using the chart as a visual aid. This will communicate to the person your personal conviction about this process and make it feel far more relational than 'instructional.'

A quick summary would look like this:

1. The way dating is practiced in our culture has resulted in hurtful and broken relationships.
2. An alternative to dating without a plan, is the Five Dating Levels. Each level has clear guidelines about how to interact and what degree of commitment is implied.

3. The success of these principles depends upon something called the Truth Triangle.
4. I have decided to start dating according to these principles because I believe it will minimize confusion, increase fun, prevent misunderstandings, avoid damaged friendships, and provide a better foundation for any relationship that may become more serious.

Here are a few tips to make this conversation easier:
- **Relax.** You are being wise and doing a good thing.
- **Breathe.** Take a deep breath and let it out slowly. This will relieve internal tension and make it easier to talk calmly.
- **Smile and just start talking.** Once you get going, momentum will carry you along.

Conversation 101

Now let's forget about "the talk." Some people have trouble just making conversation with a person of the opposite sex. It is no secret that some people are natural-born social butterflies, and others struggle to simply show up and say hello. In extreme cases, some people experienced severe taunting and ridicule as kids and are stunted in their social development. Only the loving and patient acceptance of a few compassionate people can draw a person like this out of their protective shell and convince them to try again with older and more mature people.

Many, like myself, are merely more introverted and are not naturally strong in social small talk, so they struggle when meeting new people. If you identify with this, perhaps the following suggestions will be helpful to you in getting out there and mixing it up, especially with the social small talk part of the process.

Think of conversation as game of tennis. When a person makes a comment or asks a question, it's as if he or she has hit the ball across the net to you; it's up to you to return the serve. However, this is just a warm-up volley, not an actual match. You don't want to hit the ball so hard that the other person can't return it. You want to lob your answer back so it's easy for them to hit it. Even if you're just making small talk, conversation is about keeping the ball in play. It takes two people for it to work. It may help you to know that one of the most effective secrets to conversation is to get the other person talking about himself or herself. Then you simply have to be a good listener. That's why I advise you to have several good questions memorized and ready.

> Even if you're just making small talk, conversation is about keeping the ball in play. It takes two people for it to work. . . . The most effective secret to conversation is to get the other person talking about himself or herself. Then you simply have to be a good listener.

Make a list of five to seven questions dealing with topics covering family, work, sports, hobbies, travel, politics, religion, and current events. Make sure each question is worded in such a way that it will be difficult for someone to just answer yes or no. Then, (and this is important) for each question, write two or three follow-up questions by considering the various responses that might be given. Here's an example:

Starter Question:
- What do you enjoy most about your work?

Follow-up Questions:
- Have you always been in your present career or did you do something else previously?
- Is this something you see yourself doing until you retire, or do you have a different second career dream?

The point is not to attempt to script an entire conversation, but just to get some conversational momentum going. Typically, if you can get a person talking about a particular topic long enough to answer two or three questions, you will reach sharing momentum and the conversation will become much easier. Also, as you listen, the other person will share about interesting events, places, and experiences, which will allow you to ask even better follow-up questions and lead the conversation into even more interesting directions. There are many good resources available to help you develop the art of conversation, which will make developing healthy relationships much easier![8]

A Good Foundation

Once you and the person you want to go out with are on the same page it is easy to move forward on Level One dates. If the relationship grows, you have a common language for clarifying how and when you may be ready to move to a higher level of commitment. In the next section and beyond, we will talk about the importance of checking in with one another to ensure that both of the people in a dating relationship have similar expectations and have their Truth Triangles in balance. The foundation for that kind of clear, open communication is laid here at Level One.

CHAPTER NINE

Frequently Asked Questions for Level One

Dating Lie #9: All the "good ones" are already taken.

You probably still have some questions about Level One dating. In this chapter I will address a few of the most common.

Question 1: What Are Some Ways for Me to Get a Date?

This question often conjures up awkward or frustrating memories of dating misadventures, but the answer is a matter of common sense. The following are some ways you can get a date. There are other ways of course. You could go to a singles' bar, for instance, but I wouldn't recommend it. I consider these four methods to be acceptable, although some are definitely better than others.

1. **Invite a group of people to some social event.** This environment feels safer. Because there are multiple people, there are no obvious pairings. By having many people over for a social function, attractions can happen without the stress and pressure of a one-on-one situation. The interaction allows the process of discovery to happen naturally.

2. **Use a dating service.** Some people have had success with this method. But whether you use a dating service to find someone or meet a person in a chat room, please heed this *strong* warning. The Dating Levels cannot be circumvented successfully. Admittedly, an occasional couple gets lucky, but they still have to go through the discovery process of the Bonding Stages to develop true intimacy. The sad reality is that far too often people act hastily because the other person says all the right things during their online interactions. Remember, anyone can seem better than they are over the Internet. It is a wonderful tool, but it is only a tool. Sooner or later real people have to do real things and experience real life if each is going to discover what the other is really like. Please be careful. If you meet someone on the Internet, insist that they follow the Dating Levels to ensure a good healthy bonding process. If they really are the right one, they will be glad to do what is best for you as a couple.

3. **Accept a friend's invitation to go on a blind date.** If it is a *really* good friend, this might be a fine idea, but beware! When I was fifteen, the girlfriend of a buddy of mine called and asked if I would go on a blind date with her cousin. This double date seemed harmless to me, after all, my buddy's girlfriend was really cute. Well, her cousin was cute—for a ten-year-old! Luckily for this young girl, my momma raised me right. I treated her with the utmost respect and kindness and made the best of a bad situation. I know many claim to have found the love of their life in this way, but for every person claiming a good experience, there are ten others claiming nightmares.

4. **Ask someone out!** Profound isn't it? Seriously, look around at work, in your neighborhood, or at church and

ask someone for a Level One date. Remember, at Level One, attraction is not required, only the desire and ability to go have fun. You can do that with lots of people! Go have some fun and see whom else God brings across your path in the process.

I know that many women have a big problem with asking a man out on a date. They view it as too forward and also prefer that men take the lead, which they should. But let me remind you that a Level One date is very different from a Level Two date. Most people think dating starts at Level Two, so this is not as forward as it may seem. Certainly, you can maintain your commitment not to ask a guy out on a Level One date, but remember two things:

1. **Guys are terrible at getting your hints.** We men may be oblivious to what seems obvious to you (and every other woman in the room). You may feel like you are throwing yourself at a guy in a conversation, but unless you jumped across the table and kissed him, he may not have understood that you were trying to let him know of your interest. Part of that may be cluelessness, but part of it is probably self-protection too. Not wanting to be rejected, he may convince himself that he's only imagining you're interested. So if you are not going to ask guys out at all, you better come up with more obvious ways of letting a guy know that you'd love for him to ask you out. Most guys won't ask unless they think they have a good chance at hearing a yes!

2. **If you eliminate this option, you are left with group events, dating services, and blind dates.** Are you sure you want to do that?

Question 2: How Do I Handle the Mystery of Attraction?

The mystery of attraction has existed as long as men and women have been living on earth. At the highest level is the mystery of why you can be attracted to a person and your best friend standing next to you can be totally neutral or even turned off by the same person. Attraction is different for everyone, and while there are some general standards of beauty in our culture, once you get into specifics, all bets are off. There is no way to completely understand why you are attracted to one person and not attracted to another. But you can understand your own attraction grid enough to make wise decisions.

> Studying yourself and asking good questions can enable you to gain a reasonably good understanding of your attraction grid and how it influences your relationships.

Your attraction grid is your unique set of likes and dislikes that have an impact on who you find attractive. It develops as multiple factors influence it over time. Things such as early family memories, past experiences, learned patterns, internal nuances of the soul, cultural images, and even peer influence have varying degrees of impact. Studying yourself and asking good questions can enable you to gain a reasonably good understanding of your attraction grid and how it influences your relationships. Think of your attraction grid as a pair of eyeglasses. These glasses are relationally tinted so that they affect everyone you see. They can function like sunglasses and screen out the light of certain types of people so that they are barely noticed. The also can function like magnifying glasses and make people who match the attraction tinting literally look larger than life when you see them. These are the first people you will notice at a party and you will be drawn to them.

Like any tool, the attraction grid can be used for good or evil. Negative relational consequences can occur when the attraction grid has been damaged or if the lenses have become fogged up or distorted. This can happen when you interact with dysfunctional people or when you allow worldly values to fog your grid. Either way, the only solution is a relational eye exam and ultimately new lenses. For example, maybe you tend to repeatedly get the same negative results in your relationships. To an outside observer, it may be obvious that the last three people you dated were all alike—only the names and faces were different. This is likely a sign that your attraction grid has been damaged and is causing you to be continually attracted to the wrong type of person. In extreme cases, a damaged attraction grid can lead a person from one abusive relationship to another. In more subtle forms, it shows up in self-defeating behaviors of someone who pursues people who simply don't align with his or her values, goals, lifestyle, and perspectives.

> The most effective way to change or fix any distortions on your attraction grid is to compare what you think about God, yourself, and others with the Word of God.

In the latter situation, you and the people you date may like each other, and you may have fun, but there is a limit to how far the relationship can go. This may be fine for someone with no interest in marriage, but for most people it creates a frustrating cycle of investing years in different relationships only to hit a wall at some point because they are stuck in a negative pattern. The most effective way to change or fix any distortions on your attraction grid is to compare what you think about God, yourself, and others with the Word of God. Anything that disagrees with God's Word must be renounced and replaced with the truth. This process of renewing the mind (see

Romans 12:1–2 and 2 Corinthians 10:3–5) takes time, but it will take effect and change your perceptions for the better. In addition, it helps when a few trusted friends are aware of what God has shown you; they can hold you accountable when you try to replace truth with lies.

It is also important to understand that other people's attraction grids affect how they perceive you. Many singles are frustrated because they have been so busy chasing the image in their attraction grid that they have not given any thought to what they are projecting to others. The reality is that there are some things about your appearance and personality that you simply can't change. But there are some things all of us can change. I recommend to everyone that they select a trusted friend of the opposite sex (someone toward whom you have no romantic attraction) and ask that person to give you honest evaluation and feedback about anything they think members of the opposite sex would like and dislike about you.

> A simple "no thank you" said with love and respect is a sufficient answer for declining a date. There is no need to come up with reasons that you think will somehow protect a person's feelings.

Many times people are surprised about simple things that are easily fixed (such as hygiene, outdated hairstyles or clothing, conversation nuances, etc.) which have made them less than attractive to others. Anything that you feel is reasonable and biblical can be corrected, and new opportunities often present themselves. A common problem I've seen is with older singles (especially men) who don't realize that they are still looking through an attraction grid from their twenties. Except in rare cases, these individuals have an unrealistic perception of themselves and are continually frustrated when the much younger people they are attracted to do not reciprocate the interest. Long ago I was a bartender, and I observed this sad ritual firsthand night after night for years. A humble but healthy dose of reality that causes you to reevaluate and reset your attraction grid can set you free from such misery.

Question 3: How Do I Keep from Hurting the Other Person's Feelings in Level One Dating?

In this section I have emphasized the casual nature of Level One dating. No commitment, no implied next date, no hard feelings. That's what makes Level One dating so revolutionary. But because Level One dating runs so counter to what people are accustomed to, singles often ask me about the potential for hurting other people's feelings. After all, we're accustomed to feeling hurt when people say, "No thank you," or when they choose not to continue a dating relationship. If you are concerned about protecting other people's feelings (or your own) in a dating situation, you need to remember the following truth: protecting the feelings of others is only possible when you have a balanced Truth Triangle. It's true that honesty can hurt sometimes. *But it doesn't hurt nearly as much as dishonesty.*

Consider this verse from James: "Above all, my brothers, do not swear—not by heaven or by earth or by anything else. Let your 'Yes' be yes, and your 'No,' no, or you will be condemned" (James 5:12). One sure way to hurt people's feelings is to break your promises. People who have the habit of making promises they don't keep are not good candidates for permanent relationships. Another habit this verse addresses is the inexplicable compulsion some people feel to give lots of reasons (often rather lame ones) for why they do or don't want to do something. A simple "no thank you" said with love and respect is a sufficient answer for declining a date. There is no need to come up with reasons that you think will somehow protect a person's feelings. The excuses are rarely believable except to an unstable person who will probably continue asking until you get frustrated enough to give them a strong no. Unfortunately, by then your earlier attempts at protecting them will probably cause more pain than a simple no would have done at the beginning. *Yes and no are complete sentences!*

The following passage from Ephesians is one of the best overall descriptions of healthy communication in the Bible:

> Therefore each of you must put off falsehood and speak truthfully to his neighbor, for we are all members of one body. "In your anger do not sin": Do not let the sun go down while you are still angry, and do not give the devil a foothold. He who has been stealing must steal no longer, but must work, doing something useful with his own hands, that he may have something to share with those in need. Do not let any unwholesome talk come out of your mouths, but only what is helpful for building others up according to their needs, that it may benefit those who listen. And do not grieve the Holy Spirit of God, with whom you were sealed for the day of redemption. Get rid of all bitterness, rage and anger, brawling and slander, along with every form of malice. Be kind and compassionate to one another, forgiving each other, just as in Christ God forgave you. (Ephesians 4:25–32)

The exhortations to be direct, truthful, wholesome, and edifying are timeless principles that make for success in all types of relationships whether they are romantic, friendly, or professional. The additional instruction not to allow the enemy to poison your soul with anger and bitterness is especially wise. I can't tell you how sad it is to be at a funeral and observe the negative interactions of family and friends who have been stewing in age-old disagreements. They're literally carrying them to the grave. If you follow the Lord's advice in this passage in all your relationships, you will live and die with peace of mind.

Human beings are messy and dating—even when you follow the Five Dating Levels—will inevitably bring up moments that will hurt. Though you should be as kind as you can, in the end you aren't responsible for other people's feelings. More to the point, sometimes being kind requires that you say something that hurts another person's feelings. Your responsibility is to be direct, honest, kind, and patient in all your interactions, even those uncomfortable interactions that require you to say, "No, thank you." God wants you to live with such integrity that even if another person is disappointed when you say no, he or she will have to say that you've done nothing wrong.

> Though you should be as kind as you can, in the end you aren't responsible for other people's feelings. More to the point, sometimes being kind requires that you say something that hurts another person's feelings.

However, saying no isn't why you date. You go on Level One dates because you're looking for a person you can say yes to repeatedly. The goal of Level One dating is to find a person with whom you can move to Level Two.

Moving Forward

How do you know when it's time to move from Level One to Level Two? Consider the following questions before taking the next step:

1. Does this person inspire you to draw closer to God?
2. How strong is your attraction to this person:
    a. Spiritually?
    b. Mentally?
    c. Emotionally?
    d. Physically?
3. Is your Truth Triangle in balance?
4. Do either of you have a poor self-image?

Dating Because It's You

It's funny how our vision seems to be perfectly clear when it comes to other people's faults, but we tend not to see our own. When we begin dating others, the annoying aspects of both people begin to surface. No relationship is free from this reality. So what makes people want to move into more committed levels of relationship? Simply put, couples who have a lot in common and share a strong attraction tend to be able to overlook the downsides of each other's personalities. It is the mystery of attraction that causes people to move into Level Two dating.

Dating at Level Two is time centered, which means it requires getting to know each other better over the course of multiple dates. The key issue is that both people honestly acknowledge that there is enough attraction to warrant spending more time together. For example, my first date with my wife was a dinner party with a few other people that she had invited me to attend. We ate dinner, talked, and played games. I had a good time and felt attraction for her. Based on what I had learned about her from that event, combined with my interactions with her in our social group for a couple of years, I felt I had sufficiently tested that attraction to call and ask her on another date. A few dates later, I let her know that I was attracted to her and wanted to continue dating occasionally to see what might develop.

To acknowledge that you are attracted to a person is to make yourself vulnerable. That means you have to accept the increased risk of being hurt. After all, every dating relationship has only two possible conclusions–either you get married, or you break up. And you already know which of those conclusions is the most common.

CHAPTER TEN

Defining Level Two

Dating Lie #10: Wait for them to say it first, if you ask, you'll scare them off.

At Level One, you split your time between group dates and one-on-one dates. This gives you some time for undistracted conversation but not too much time alone. Once you move to Level Two, don't neglect group dates. You can learn a lot about another person by seeing how he or she interacts with others. I've heard it said that if you want to know what a man is really like, observe him with a child, a waiter, and a flat tire. The perspective input of others is critical; without significant interaction with groups of friends, you will not have access to this important information.

At Level Two, the relationship is still not exclusive. You could be at Level Two with one person and Level One with another. While some people prefer to date only one person at a time, others can manage the relational complexity of more than one. It is probably not wise, however, to attempt to date two different people at Level Two due to the amount of time needed and the type of bonding allowed; but if you can handle it without hurt or confusion, dating one person at Level Two and one or two others at Level One is just fine.

Up the Escalator—Level Two

Hopefully your dating life will consist of more than trips to the mall! But for the purpose of illustration, let's see what Level Two of our imaginary relational shopping mall has to offer.

Unlike the Level One date described earlier, the two of you ride to the mall together this time. Because you have already spent many dates walking around the first floor, you agree that it is time to step on the escalator of commitment and ride up to the second level (Level Two). While you still desire to have fun like you did on the first floor, the acknowledgment of real attraction creates a greater sense of risk and pressure.

In a moment of spontaneity, the two of you step into one of the photo booths and take a series of silly photos together. You laugh about them as you continue exploring this new level of the mall. Because you are now acknowledging that you are together (though not exclusive), it seems natural to have such a photo to put in your room or in your wallet. You don't mind if people ask about your relationship because you have agreed about where you are. You tell friends that you are not going steady but that you do think there might be potential so you are spending more time together to see how things progress. You can even tell this to someone who may ask you on a Level One date. This allows you to interact freely and without presumption or fear.

As you walk down the mall, you reach out and hold hands. This hand-to-hand contact in private and public is the next stage of bonding. Though the skin-to-skin contact is exciting, the main purpose at this point is to make a social statement. It communicates to others that you are together on this date and that they should not interfere. You are willing to be identified as being with the other person, and that in itself is an important statement of value. The desire kindled by multiple Level One dates and talking on the phone for hours on end in the previous stage is rewarded with the sheer joy of being in such close contact.

You stop for a snack in the food court. The person who initiated the date offers to pay. While it is fine for one to pay for the other, occasionally you go dutch treat just to minimize obligation.

After one or more dates at Level Two, communication about how you are balancing your Truth Triangles becomes vitally important. Once you have moved to Level Two, you have an obligation either to continue going out or to honestly and clearly state why you don't believe you should continue dating them at that level. Since attraction has previously been acknowledged, you are obligated to politely explain why things have changed. Since attraction is mysterious, it is often found to be less powerful than originally believed when tested over time.

> Staying connected requires intentionality.

If, however, the attraction remains or grows, communication is even more complicated. Forgive the silly example, but imagine standing in the mall shoe store. Your date wanders a few rows over to another section of the store. Twenty minutes later you realize that you are no longer together, and the racks of shoes keep you from seeing one another. So you call out and your date answers. You follow one another's voices until you find each other in the store. This illustrates how easily drift happens in a relationship. Nobody is trying to drift. Nobody is mad, nor has either party even lost interest in the other. It's just that, whatever the attraction between two people, and whatever interests they share, men and women simply have different interests and needs. That's not a bad thing. It just means that staying connected requires intentionality.

When the drift is minor, achieving reconnection is relatively easy. But when the distance is greater, it gets more complicated. For instance, if the woman is standing in the shoe store looking at new pumps while the man wanders over to the sporting goods store at the other end of the mall, the distance is very real. Now she has to take out her cell phone and call to find out where he is. By stating where she is and asking him where he is, the two of them are able to determine an appropriate meeting place to reconnect and continue their date.

When you speak the truth in love, you establish a firm foundation that will keep you from being blown back and forth by the changing winds of doctrine—or emotions, or physical desires.

Sometimes, one person may emotionally wander back down to Level One, which creates a multidimensional gap. If neither person pulls out the "cell phone" to reestablish connection, they could spend weeks wandering up and down two levels of the mall and never find one another.

Here's another analogy to help clarify. Picture two submarines moving together in the ocean from one location to another. If either of them veers off even one degree in a different direction, over the course of time they will be miles apart. They can end up pointing in different directions and even be at different depths. To rectify this tendency to drift, submarines use sonar and a process called pinging. As sound waves go through the water and bounce off the metal hulls, they create a pinging sound that enables the submarines to locate one another in terms of depth, direction, and speed.

Hopefully, these analogies and their application are obvious. Once you are at Level Two, both parties must be intentional about periodically checking in and discussing whether you are on the same page or not and whether your Truth Triangles are staying balanced and in harmony with each other. If one or both of you are struggling with thoughts, feelings, or behaviors, then talking it out, defining new and clear agreements, and recommitting to the process must happen. This is the only way to move through the relational process together in terms of speed, depth, and direction.

The Bible makes it clear that open, honest, and loving communication is not just important but commanded.

> Then we will no longer be infants, tossed back and forth by the waves, and blown here and there by every wind of teaching and by the cunning and craftiness of men in their deceitful scheming. Instead, speaking the truth in love, we will in all things grow up into him who is the Head, that is, Christ. (Ephesians 4:14–15)

I realize Paul wasn't talking about Level Two dating when he told the Ephesians to speak the truth in love. But when you speak the truth in love, you establish a firm foundation that will keep you from being blown back and forth by the changing winds of doctrine—or emotions, or physical desires. And that foundation of truth will also protect you from deceit, including the deceit of a culture that has a warped view of male-female relationships.

That's what's at stake in the check-in, and I strongly recommend that the man initiate this at least once per month. It is also acceptable for the woman to initiate, especially if she is struggling, or he has been lax in doing so.

Two More Bonding Stages at Level Two

At Level One, the bonding stages—eye-to-body, eye-to-eye, voice-to-voice—don't involve physical contact. There is no commitment, so there is no contact. It's all about the Truth

Triangle and keeping behaviors (and thoughts and feelings) in line with your commitments. There *is* a commitment involved at Level Two, but because it is a limited commitment, the allowable physical contact is limited as well. Hand-to-hand contact, as we have already discussed, is an outward sign of the interest that a Level Two couple has acknowledged.

> To end the relationship now hurts, but not nearly as much as ending it at one of the higher dating levels.

After several Level Two dates and hopefully at least one check-in, it may be appropriate for the man to put his arm around the woman's shoulder. While not yet an embrace or hug, arm-to-shoulder contact is a significant step forward in indicating a sense of ownership on the part of both people. I don't mean that either person owns the other. I mean that together the man and the woman own their relationship and take responsibility for it. At this bonding stage, it is more difficult for another person to break in or intrude, as the physical contact now includes the shoulders and arms, not just the hands. Walking arm-to-shoulder, you still spend your time facing outward as you walk along observing and discussing the world around you. You enjoy each other's company and develop a sense of comfort as you test the waters of these newfound feelings.

A few more dates and check-ins allow the process to take you to the last bonding safe spot of Level Two. The weeks and months of conversation, fun, sharing, discussing, clarifying, and checking in have produced a steady confidence in the potential of this relationship. So as you walk along, suddenly it just seems right: the man puts his arm around the woman's waist. Now things begin to get much more serious. While there is still no significant face-to-face contact, the bodies are drawn closer together and the arms move to the waist—an area typically not touched by others.

One of the natural results of arm-to-waist contact (you can observe it for yourself the next time you see a couple walking with their arms around one another's waists) is that the couple's heads drop down as they walk. They are no longer focused outwardly on the world, but inward toward each other. Now the conversation is more private, in more hushed tones, and begins to cover many topics at a deeper level. Personal disclosures begin to come forth as trust has grown.

At this stage, deep in Level Two, you must discuss life vision and dreams—at least in enough detail to determine if moving forward is wise. This brings up an important point: the result of this increased closeness may be that you realize that you *don't* have a future together. Remember, though you've increased your commitment at Level Two, you haven't committed to begin a new life together. What you've really committed to is an honest assessment of where you stand and where your relationship might be going. If you discover the relationship has nowhere to go, that's okay. To end the relationship now hurts, but not nearly as much as ending it at one of the higher dating levels.

When the Dating Journey Ends

As I have already said, every relationship has only two possible outcomes, either the couple gets married or they break up. This is unavoidable, but it doesn't have to be as difficult and damaging as most people make it. By following the parameters of the Dating Levels and maintaining a balanced Truth Triangle, a couple can end their relationship with honor, grace, and peace. The monthly check-ins provide the necessary temperature and heart readings to make such decisions amicably and decisively. When such a conclusion is reached, the following things should be considered:

1. Define the new boundaries of your relationship in terms of new ways to interact.

2. *Be careful not to talk too much until time has passed to help emotions heal.*
3. *Agree on what you both will say to other people when they ask what happened.*
4. *Don't attempt mind reading when you interact with the other person in public. In other words, don't assume you know what they are thinking, especially if you imagine they are thinking something bad.*
5. *Don't avoid each other in public; any awkwardness will pass in time.*
6. *Pray for each other's future relationships to be blessed by God.*
7. *Think about the lessons you learned that will help with your future relationships.*

The risk in this situation is higher proportionate to how long the relationship has lasted, but the principles still apply. If you have lived with integrity and followed God's design, then whatever sadness results from your decision will be healed more quickly and easily because of the foundation you laid. Honest, direct, kind, and edifying words of appreciation soften the reality that the relationship should not go further. Mutual respect for each other before and during the relationship now makes ending the relationship without bitterness very possible. A friendship can be salvaged and the social community can focus on supporting the healing instead of choosing sides of a conflict. You can't avoid sadness and disappointment—especially if one person feels the dating relationship should end when the other doesn't—but you can avoid bitterness and broken community. If you follow God's process, bitterness, awkwardness, and the soap opera experience so common in our world can be tossed away once and for all. God's ways work!

The Spiritual Dimension

The Bible exhorts us to pursue spiritual depth in all our relationships. While both parties contribute to this, generally it is the man's role to take the lead in that pursuit. As a pastor, I have had countless discussions with men who wanted to take the lead spiritually, but who felt ill equipped or even incompetent to do so. While most men feel some degree of these emotions, the good news is that the solution is quite simple. I urge you to read and meditate on the following passage of Scripture:

> Be joyful always; pray continually; give thanks in all circumstances, for this is God's will for you in Christ Jesus. Do not put out the Spirit's fire; do not treat prophecies with contempt. Test everything. Hold on to the good. Avoid every kind of evil. May God himself, the God of peace, sanctify you through and through. May your whole spirit, soul and body be kept blameless at the coming of our Lord Jesus Christ. *The one who calls you is faithful and he will do it.* (1 Thessalonians 5:16–24, emphasis added)

Did you notice that last sentence? God is faithful, and he will do it. You don't feel faithful enough? Good for you for being honest. The good news is that God is faithful even when we are faithless. Leading spiritually does not mean knowing more about the Bible than your date, or being able to answer all the questions people ask. It means that you are personally committed to fully following Christ and that you show that commitment in how you invest your time, talents, and treasures. You organize your life around him and his Word. Your leadership is inviting your date to talk about such things, pray with you, and go with you as you help others. God will help you to do this, but you must take the step of faith trusting the power of his Spirit to help.

> The good news is that God is faithful even when we are faithless. Leading spiritually . . . means that you are personally committed to fully following Christ and that you show that commitment in how you invest your time, talents, and treasures.

The Physical Dimension

If you haven't already figured it out, there is no kissing in the first two dating levels. There are good spiritual, emotional, and psychological reasons for this boundary. This issue alone demonstrates how far off-track our culture has gotten. With kissing (and even sex) being encouraged on the first date or soon after, it is no wonder so many people are walking around wounded and confused. It is no wonder that so many people report a lack of connection even with people they have been with for a long time. The Bible is clear about the importance of physical boundaries. If you really care about another person, you should want to protect them and not put them in peril.

Given everything I've been saying about physical boundaries at Level Two, it may seem premature to start talking about sex. But the truth is, anytime there is skin-to-skin contact between a man and woman who are attracted to one another—even if they're only holding hands—a certain amount of sexual tension enters the equation. But even at Level Two it's important that you have a biblical view of sex.

God is all for sex but only within the confines of marriage. Read the Song of Solomon and listen to how the Word of God exalts the beauty and joy of sexual intimacy between a husband and a wife. Remember, God created sex and made it pleasurable. He is not a prude, but he is prudent and wants to bless and protect people from inappropriate bonding.

My Story

I remember early on when my wife and I were at Level Two. We had just finished dinner at my house and we went out on the back porch to talk. I felt the nudge of the Holy Spirit to pray so I nervously asked her if she would be willing to spend some time praying with me for our friends, families, and some situations in the world. That moment is permanently burned into both of our memories because God's Spirit really met us there. I believe he made that time special for Kim and me because I obeyed him and led spiritually in our relationship.

The passage below promises that God's divine power through Christ Jesus enables us to "participate in the divine nature." This means that we can have the strength and wisdom to lead as well as to overcome our tendencies toward shirking responsibility or sinking into sin.

> We can have the strength and wisdom to lead as well as to overcome our tendencies toward shirking responsibility or sinking into sin.

His divine power has given us everything we need for life and godliness through our knowledge of him who called us by his own glory and goodness. Through these he has given us his very great and precious promises, so that through them you may participate in the divine nature and escape the corruption in the world caused by evil desires. (2 Peter 1:3–4)

The goal at Level Two is to develop friendship through fun, conversation, and prayer. Spiritual discussion and prayer becomes even more important than before once the arm-to-waist bonding begins. As you walk along with heads down, sharing your hopes and dreams, you should find clear evidence that the other person is walking with God when you are not around. The other person having a personal, vibrant faith is crucial to the long-term success of a relationship. His or her involvement in church, small groups, personal devotions, prayer, and service in the community forges the kind of character that you should be looking for in a more committed relationship.

Obviously, this is true for your own life as well. Time spent talking about spiritual things, praying, and discussing ways to serve the community together will either prove the relationship can move forward or make it painfully clear that it shouldn't.

Touchstones at Level Two

At Level Two, be sure to keep the following in mind:
- **Spend time in real conversation.** *With Level Two dating the focus has to shift from just having fun to investing sufficient time to know the other person. Take care to develop a friendship and learn a wide range of general information about each other.*
- **Equally balance group time and alone time.** *Too often a couple quickly falls into the trap of spending too much time alone, which causes them to move too fast and go too deep emotionally in their conversation.*
- **Take turns paying for dates.** *When the man pays for all the dates at Level Two, it reinforces the feeling of an exclusive relationship. Take turns paying at Level Two to show a mutual desire to build the friendship. A good rule is that whoever asks, pays.*
- **Attend to the spiritual component of your relationship.** *Intentional times of prayer and discussion of Bible reading or church teaching is critical. I would caution that praying with someone can be very intimate emotionally. Prayer topics should stay at the level of the general conversation. The more intimate praying for more personal things should be saved for Level Three.*
- **Move through the Bonding Stages at an appropriate pace.** *Just because arm-to-waist contact is allowed at this level, doesn't mean it should happen immediately. Slow down even if you want to move faster. Give yourself plenty of time to enjoy just holding hands. Remember, you may come to a point soon where you discover you don't want to continue dating, and the less contact you have, the easier it is to stop. After a while you can move to arm-to-shoulder contact. Again, take your time. I typically recommend three to six months at Level Two, so save some of the physical contact for months five and six where it is better experienced.*
- **Respect physical boundaries.** *Even though it is obvious, I want to add that going beyond the physical boundaries for Level Two is extremely*

unwise. Once you begin kissing, the sexual engine really begins to rev up. Please, spare yourself the agony of violating the biblical parameters of sexual energy. If your relationship is actually a good one, it is worth the wait. If it isn't a good one, you shouldn't be going there anyway.

My Story

After I had been dating my future wife for a few months, I heard about her famous "last supper" technique she had used when she was younger to end dating relationships. My wife has a very tender and merciful heart, and the only way she could break up with someone was to make her delicious gourmet lasagna for him. I guess it was her 'relational penance' for breaking his heart. She had done this on a couple of occasions, and when I heard about it, I thought it was pretty funny. I'll never forget coming home from work one night after we were married to find lasagna on the table. My heart stopped beating for a moment. Thankfully, she wasn't going anywhere... she just likes Italian food. Whew! The moral of the story is: Be honest. Don't make it a guessing game.

CHAPTER ELEVEN

Relational Air Bubbles

Dating Lie #11: I'll never understand what causes my relationships to blow up.

When I was in college, I took a pottery course. I learned to throw pots on a potter's wheel and then fire them in the kiln to harden the clay so that the pots could be used. Sometimes, one or more of the pots would literally blow up during the firing process. This would happen because someone failed to find and remove all of the air bubbles in the clay. The air bubbles allowed steam from evaporating moisture trapped in the clay to collect and create pressure. The rapid expansion would cause an explosion, ruining the pot and sometimes a few innocent bystander pots as well.

Dating is a lot like this. Our relationships are thrown onto the dating wheel and slowly formed into some desirable shape. We put it in the kiln to harden the pot into something that will last (i.e., we move to an exclusive or permanent relationship) and boom, unresolved issues explode under the heat and pressure of life together. The relationship is ruined, and sometimes, innocent people around us are hurt as well.

It is at Level Two that a dating relationship is just starting to take shape. Here is where the patterns are set and expectations are formed. Sometimes unhealthy habits lie hidden like air bubbles in clay. This chapter is devoted to six such air bubbles that need to be addressed at Level Two before they have a chance to explode.

Air Bubble #1: Poor Communication Skills

> Instead, speaking the truth in love, we will in all things grow up into him who is the Head, that is, Christ. (Ephesians 4:15)

Although we've already discussed communication throughout the book, it is worth emphasizing that a lack of understanding about healthy communication is a major source of relational disintegration. Even the differences between how men and women communicate is a big problem. Simply observe a group of men hanging out together and compare that with how you see women interact; it is remarkably different. When you put a man and a woman into a relationship, these differences produce endless opportunities for misunderstanding, miscommunication, and frustration.

Air Bubble #2: Low Self-Esteem

> For you created my inmost being; you knit me together in my mother's womb. I praise you because I am fearfully and wonderfully made; your works are wonderful, I know that full well. My frame was not hidden from you when I was made in the secret place. When I was woven together in the depths of the earth, your eyes saw my unformed body. All the days ordained for me were written in your book before one of them came to be. (Psalm 139:13–16)

What is low self-esteem? It is an inaccurate and unbiblical perspective about your own value, ability, or potential in life. It causes you to live in fear of failure, to reject compliments, to be unwilling to receive love when it is offered, and to see yourself and life in a generally negative light. In extreme cases, people with low self-esteem will put up with abuse because they don't feel worthy of anything better. Sometimes, people who struggle with this malady will turn their frustration on others by being constantly critical in a warped attempt to make themselves feel better by putting others down.

> When a person decides to let what God says about them be more important than what others say, the result is freedom, confidence, and inner peace. Everyone wants to be liked by all, but you must understand that you can't please everyone. You have to choose.

In Psalm 139, God speaks some of the most encouraging words you will ever hear. He tells us that he made us! His description of knitting us together in our mother's womb is an amazing picture of God's intimate involvement in our lives from the moment of conception. He says we are "wonderfully made," meaning unique and special. And if that were not enough, he says all our days are written in his book—a clear statement that our lives have purpose and meaning. We are not random accidents bouncing around at the mercy of fate. He loves us and has a plan for us.

I'm definitely not a fan of the *I'm Okay, You're Okay* philosophy because it tends to promote either self-focus and introspection or leads to arrogance and denial. I am, however, a big believer in the value of knowing who you are in Christ. When a person decides to let what God says about them be more important than what others say, the result is freedom, confidence, and inner peace. Everyone wants to be liked by all, but you must understand that you can't please everyone. You have to choose.

Experience has shown me that those who choose to please God and allow him to adopt them as his children through a relationship with Jesus Christ are more able to accept their weaknesses with dignity and utilize their strengths with grace. They are confident in Christ, able to open up to others, forgive when wronged, able to weather difficulty, and demonstrate a stability that is vital to healthy relationships. Dr. Neil Anderson's book *Victory Over the Darkness* is an excellent resource to help you understand who you are in Christ. In his book, he provides a great list of Scriptures that reveal what God says about you. Below is a partial list from Dr. Anderson's book.[9]

I am accepted:
- I am God's child (John 1:12)
- I have been justified (Romans 5:1)

I am secure:
- I am free forever from condemnation (Romans 8:1–2)
- I cannot be separated from the love of God (Romans 8:35–39)

I am significant:
- I am God's workmanship (Ephesians 2:10)
- I am God's temple (1 Corinthians 3:16)

Air Bubble #3: Unrealistic Expectations

For by the grace given me I say to every one of you: Do not think of yourself more highly than you ought, but rather think of yourself with sober judgment, in accordance with the measure of faith God has given you. Just as each of us has one body with many members, and these members do not all have the same function, so in Christ we who are many form one body, and each member belongs to all the others. We have different gifts, according to the grace given us. If a man's gift is prophesying, let him use it in proportion to his faith. (Romans 12:3–6)

Romans 12 exhorts us to be realistic about our strengths and weaknesses. We should thank God for our strengths and with humility accept our weaknesses, realizing that how we are made is an integral part of God's plan. As we apply this humble and realistic acceptance to others, it frees everyone to be themselves and work together by submitting to one another's abilities and bearing one another's weaknesses.

A large percentage of the conflicts in relationships originate in the unrealistic expectations that people have. She assumed he would think and do 'A,' but he assumed that anyone would naturally think and do 'B.' And the fight begins. Often a woman has the unrealistic expectation that a man can meet all her emotional needs (absolutely not true), and when she feels let down she reacts with hurt or anger. He, feeling like he can never do enough, withdraws from her in frustration. This creates a sense of abandonment in her, so she reacts more strongly, as does he, and the cycle continues. A man, on the other hand, often has the unrealistic expectation that a woman should be able to express herself in a conversation (especially an argument) without bringing emotions into the picture to "muddy the water." Men mistakenly think that women should be content to talk about issues objectively and not have the need to talk about the relationship. After all, if they had changed their feelings about her they would tell her, right? There are many other aspects of this, but I think you get the point.

Air Bubble #4: Self-Centeredness

Since, then, you have been raised with Christ, set your hearts on things above, where Christ is seated at the right hand of God. Set your minds on things above, not on earthly things. For you died, and your life is now hidden with Christ in God. When Christ, who is your life, appears, then you also will appear with him in glory.

Put to death, therefore, whatever belongs to your earthly nature: sexual immorality, impurity, lust, evil desires and greed, which is idolatry. Because of these, the wrath of God is coming. You used to walk in these ways, in the life you once lived. But now you must rid yourselves of all such things as these: anger, rage, malice, slander, and filthy language from your lips. Do not lie to each other, since you have taken off your old self with its practices and have put on the new self, which is being renewed in knowledge in the image of its Creator. (Colossians 3:1–10)

> Only the indwelling power of the Holy Spirit can enable you to love others sacrificially, especially when they aren't reciprocating such love.

To ignore our natural tendency toward selfishness is foolish if you want healthy relationships. The Bible teaches that every person is born with a spiritual disease called sin that causes us to choose ourselves over anyone else, even God. Until this is dealt a deathblow by Jesus Christ, you will be your own worst enemy in any relationship you may have. People without a personal relationship with God can deny themselves for the sake of another up to a certain point. But when the stakes are the highest and the chips are down, they don't have the internal strength to put you or your future kids first. The selfishness of sin will win out and the relationship will either end or develop deep rifts of disconnection and disillusionment.

Besides the obvious fact that you should date people who have an active personal relationship with God, the best advice I can give you for building healthy relationships is to receive Christ as your personal Savior. Focus on learning more about God and live out what you learn.

The bottom line is that our purity is very important to God and very influential in our relationships.

Only the indwelling power of the Holy Spirit can enable you to love others sacrificially, especially when they aren't reciprocating such love. This is the glue that makes the verbal commitment "till death do us part" actually stand the test of time.

The Dating Levels provide ample time and a multitude of opportunities to see if the person you are attracted to is selfish or not. Little things matter because they prepare us to handle the bigger things. Look for joyful and sacrificial actions on their part. If you don't observe any or instead see a lot of selfishness, don't move forward in the relationship...no matter how good looking the other person may be!

Air Bubble #5: Sexual Immorality

Flee from sexual immorality. All other sins a man commits are outside his body, but he who sins sexually sins against his own body. Do you not know that your body is a temple of the Holy Spirit, who is in you, whom you have received from God? You are not your own; you were bought at a price. Therefore honor God with your body. (1 Corinthians 6:18–20)

Once we realize that our bodies are not your own, it changes our view of sexuality. We belong to God. He created us and then redeemed us from slavery to sin by purchasing us with the blood of Jesus Christ. His Spirit lives inside of those who have received him, so any use of our body literally is done with him.

He created sex and wants to bless us in marriage with it. He also understands your sexual energy and will help you redirect it toward positive things if you are not married. The bottom line is that our purity is very important to God and very influential in our relationships.

If you want to protect your partner from violating their boundaries and their conscience, you must be self-controlled. An inability to control yourself sexually is selfish (there it is again), and it creates an under-lying trust issue. Fast forward three years into marriage; your spouse had to go out of town on business, and you had a big fight before your spouse left town. In the wee hours of the morning, you remember that your spouse wasn't very good at self-control with you before marriage. You wonder what will happen if they meet someone on the plane who makes them feel better than they felt when they left the house in a huff. This is just one small example of the negative consequences that come from violating God's parameters for sexual intimacy. It sets in motion all manner of problems and relational distortions.

> An inability to control yourself sexually is selfish, and it creates an underlying trust issue.

Air Bubble #6: Ignoring God's Word and Making Foolish Choices

> To the Jews who had believed him, Jesus said, "If you hold to my teaching, you are really my disciples. Then you will know the truth, and the truth will set you free." (John 8:31–32)

The ability to discern the truth in any situation and make good choices is a critical skill in life and in relationships. This is another reason why it is so important to have a relationship with God. The Holy Spirit promises to help us understand all things about Jesus Christ, which enables us to make wise decisions and live well.

Jesus said in the verses above, "Then you will know the truth, and the truth will set you free." God has given us freedom of will, but many of us live in bondage to worldly philosophies and opinions, which produce nothing but rotten fruit. The Word of God not only shows us the truth about spiritual things, but also about all kinds of practical things. The Bible gives great instruction about relationships, communication, finances, family boundaries, handling stress, dealing with loss and disappointment, and even making wise choices. The following are a few of the choices you must make:

You decide *who* you will date
> Will you date people who share your values and perspective on life, or people you know in your heart are not good for you?

You decide *how* you will date
> Will you date the same old way of the world or by God's relational design? Will you rush into physical intimacy or follow the Bonding Stages and Dating Levels? Will you spend all your time alone together and isolate yourselves from friends and family, or will you choose to balance your time so that you can get perspective and input?

You decide *who* you will marry and *when* you will do so
> Are these important facts enough to make you stop and assess your need for wisdom to make good choices? Remember, your choices have a huge impact on the quality of your life experience.

At this point I want to talk a little more about recovering from divorce. If you've experienced this painful trauma, I strongly recommend you get professional Christian counseling to help process the grief, and I recommend you find a local chapter of the DivorceCare ministry in your area. They have an excellent biblical program that has helped thousands around the country not only heal, but learn how to avoid similar mistakes in the future. One or more of the six air bubbles I just discussed are usually at the heart of any divorce. Add fighting over money, which flows out of selfishness, and you cover the gamut. If you've been divorced, or if you have been through some pretty devastating breakups, I encourage you to go back and reread this chapter. Meditate on the verses and teaching. Make notes about what God is saying to you. Then contact a counselor or some other type of support and let them help you remove these air bubbles from your relational life.

Moving Forward

How do you know when it's time to move from Level Two to Level Three? Consider the following questions before taking the next step:

1. How have you grown spiritually, individually, and as a couple since dating?
2. How strong is your attraction to this person now compared with your initial attraction?
   a. Spiritually
   b. Mentally
   c. Emotionally
   d. Physically
3. Is your Truth Triangle in balance?

4. Does this person appear to be consistently stable emotionally?
5. Do your friends like this person?
6. Does this person respect the physical boundaries of the Dating Levels?

LEVEL THREE
Dating with the Future in View

To love at all is to be vulnerable. Love anything, and your heart will certainly be wrung and possibly broken. If you want to make sure of keeping it intact, you must give your heart to no one, not even to an animal. Wrap it carefully around with hobbies and little luxuries; avoid all entanglements; lock it up safe in the casket or coffin of your selfishness. But in that casket—safe, dark, motionless, airless—it will change. It will not be broken; it will become unbreakable, impenetrable, irredeemable.

—C. S. Lewis, *The Four Loves*[10]

Level Three dating is far more relationship focused than the previous two levels. Level One focuses mostly on fun whereas Level Two focuses more on spending enough time together to determine if exclusivity is warranted. Level Three has a stronger focus on the official relationship and how it might develop into something permanent. Some would call this "going steady." The relationship is exclusive because the couple has gained enough confidence in its potential to forgo dating others. They are also willing to risk the much greater level of hurt that would result if the relationship ends later on. Investing lots of time and energy and sharing vulnerability is the best way to build a healthy relationship, but it also creates a higher risk that your heart could be broken. That is why I recommend that a couple date at Levels One and Two for at least three to six months before moving to Level Three. Done properly, it is always worth the wait!

CHAPTER TWELVE

Defining Level Three

Dating Lie #12: All you need is love.

I had just finished teaching a Sunday school class for singles when two of the leaders in our singles ministry approached me. He was tall, analytical, and even-tempered, while she was bubbly, creative, and brimming with life. I had noticed them spending time together for several months and had counseled with each of them about their questions on the Dating Levels. As they stood there, I wondered what they wanted to say to me. He looked down at her and said, "Do you want to do it, or should I?" She smiled up at him and said, "Go for it."

"Well, we did it," he said. "We officially moved to Level Three!" This was a major step for this young man. He had married and divorced very early in life and was extremely gun-shy about any future committed relationships. He had come to know Christ a few years prior to this conversation and realized that he had a lot of issues to work through. He had diligently pursued God and grown by leaps and bounds. Life was good for him, and he was truly content for the first time. He had made lots of friends in the church, had a job he liked, and was growing as a leader. This relationship had caught him by surprise. He had moved slowly but was thankful for the teaching on the

Dating Levels. It provided him with the concrete and objective perspective his analytical nature needed to muster the courage to commit to an exclusive relationship. Several months later, I had the privilege of performing their wedding ceremony. It was a joyous occasion.

What Does Dating with the Future in View Look Like?

So you find yourself at our imaginary relational mall again with the person you've been dating for five or six months. (After all, this mall has a special place in your heart; remember your first date here?) You're walking toward the escalator leading to Level Three, your arms around each other's waists, with a mixture of excitement and anxiety. Your group of friends waves at you from Level Two. You both will continue to come back downstairs to spend time with these friends, but not quite as often, as you will be spending more of your time with one another up on Level Three.

At the top of the escalator you see a whole new variety of stores. Most of them sell items that would be a little too personal to shop for with a member of the opposite sex on the lower levels. You stroll into the Pottery Barn and spend time looking at the various household gadgets and furnishings. Discussions about your personal styles in the kitchen, living room, and throughout the house make you think about possible future purchases you may make together as husband and wife. You both stop and acknowledge the fact that it is fun to think about such things but still too early to dwell on them. You agree to rebalance your Truth Triangles by putting those thoughts aside, and you continue strolling through the mall.

Next you find yourself inside the Macy's department store. Together you roam through the various sections of men's and women's clothing. You take turns waiting while the other tries on clothes, giving feedback as to which items would make a good purchase. This up close and personal interaction means that you will be gazing on each other's bodies (clothed of course) in ways not previously allowed. You will be risking misunderstandings and hurt feelings as you give feedback about how things look on one another and whether or not they are too expensive. You will learn a lot about each other's temperament as such adventures allow you to find out who is detail oriented, who is on time, who is late, who is tactful, who is more abrasive, and other such things that couples need to know before marriage.

Around dinnertime, the two of you meet up with your parents to eat. This time spent with each other's families allows them to give you input on the relationship and also prepares them to celebrate with you should the relationship progress to an engagement. It also allows you to see issues that exist in your date's family of origin. What baggage can be expected? How does her dad treat her mom? How does he relate with his brother or sister? Family dynamics have a huge influence on a couple's relationship. No family is perfect, but it is important that you and your date learn how to handle any dysfunctional tendencies within family systems. Things like passive aggressive behavior, persistent negativity and criticism, controlling behaviors and words, and overstepping of bounds all put pressure on your relationship. At the very least, both you and your date need to be confident that you are able to put up the necessary boundaries to protect yourselves personally and as a couple, neither being drawn into family dysfunction nor being overly agitated by it. Ideally, you will want to be able to speak the truth in love to family members so that destructive behaviors can be squelched.

You also need to consider your compatibility with your date's family. Do they seem to welcome you? Do you fit in or not? Is conversation easy or strained? Is their value system evident? If so, does it seem to match with yours? How is this family similar to your own, and how is it different? Being welcomed and comfortable in your date's family system is pretty important. Sometimes the family is so dysfunctional that fitting in is not healthy. In this case, it's likely that your date has already had to put some pretty strong boundaries in place to honor his or her parents without perpetuating negative behaviors. However, most of the time, the family is healthy enough that regular interaction with them will be possible and necessary, so getting a clear sense of comfort and belonging is important. Be sure to look at value issues such as standard of living, views of God, and attitudes toward people of different races or economic status. Hopefully you'll feel that in many ways this family could be your family, which is not to say that this family is perfect. All of this is learned in the context of relaxed social gatherings.

Before dessert comes, your date's coworker walks up to the table and says hello. How do they interact? Are they warm? Polite? Tense? All during the dinner you continue to go through the bonding stages you have already covered. You are noticing new things about each other, the eye tag and blushing still happens, the thrill of hearing their voice. You hold hands, then an arm goes around the shoulders. You feel only a brief moment of awkwardness at this kind of affection being seen by family and coworkers.

After everyone says their goodbyes, the two of you decide to continue on alone walking through the mall as the others go home. After an hour or so of enjoying the depth of friendship, understanding, and mutual love and respect that has developed so far, you decide to get a private booth in the back of the restaurant for another cup of coffee. You delve into detailed talks about your life goals, your attitudes about children, your desired standard of living, and your personal value systems until you realize it's really late. The time just seems to fly when you talk about things like this.

After a quiet but comfortable ride home, you walk together to the doorstep, and you look into one other's eyes. You're trying to read something there. Are you both feeling the same thing? Finally, after months of patient relationship building, the kissing can begin! You are at the next bonding stage: face-to-face. The old song says "a kiss is just a kiss," but that's not true at all. Kissing allows a reasonable expression of the normal intimate desires that have been growing in your hearts, and it also serves a very practical purpose: it forges a very strong emotional bond that helps the couple weather difficult times. God's design is perfect—romantic and practical. Because so much has been invested up to this point, you can now communicate volumes without even speaking simply by reading each other's faces, glances, and mannerisms. There is a knowing of each other that, while it has not gone beyond first base so to speak, is still very intimate emotionally.

The next bonding stage, hand-to-head, often follows quickly and naturally. If you doubt that this is a legitimate stage, try this experiment. Walk up to someone you don't know and reach out your hand to touch his or her face. Be prepared for an unpleasant reaction. You don't allow people to touch your face and/or head without a good reason. It is a natural instinct due to the vulnerability of the skull and face. Only a doctor, a hairdresser, or a trusted friend is allowed such access. This type of intimate touch occurs most often when a couple is looking into one other's eyes, sharing a moment, and stroking the hair. It is yet another precursor to the future and more specific sexual contact, which by this point is becoming a strong desire in your hearts. This desire is not evil or sinful but normal according to God's design. The key is to control your desire and follow God's commands to wait for your wedding night, where it can be unleashed with unashamed glory.

The final bonding stage at Level Three follows right on the heels of this one. This hand-to-body stage involves a memorization and appreciation of a person's body in terms of how it looks, feels, and how they fill a room. I'm not talking about getting naked here, but rather simple things such as rubbing of the neck and back, noticing a mole or pattern of freckles, becoming familiar with the texture of the other person's hair, recognizing how they walk, sit, or stand.

Before you say goodbye for the evening, you pray together, thanking God for his many blessings and asking for his continued guidance and protection for your relationship. You commit yourselves to the greatest good of the other person – even if that means breaking up. Your time together has created not just a romance but a friendship that must be protected. You have a friendship that moves you to deny yourself for the sake of the other person; to put their needs ahead of your own. You have a desire to see them become all that God intended. A final quick kiss and he gets into his car and drives away while you lock your door and spend some time cherishing the events of the evening.

Sexual Time Bombs

The bonding stages that you go through in Level Three are wonderful. They are also dangerous. For some people, kissing and nonsexual intimate interaction creates a sexual tension that is too difficult to control. For others, it creates too much distraction from other aspects of the relationship. The lesson here should be obvious. By God's design, these stages are meant to help a couple connect first in spirit, then connect at the soul level (mind, will, emotions), and finally to connect physically with their bodies in sexual union. The process is real in dating and necessary to create and maintain a good marriage. If at any time the process creates too much tension or momentum toward crossing physical boundaries, the couple should step back, catch their breath, and move more slowly. This act of self-control protects the relationship and develops deep trust for one another. But without such self-control, without real intentionality, the appropriate intimacy of Level Three can be like a ticking time bomb.

Every major city has a bomb squad. These brave men and women come onto the scene when suspicious packages are discovered in public places. In this age of terrorism, the threat is prevalent and constant. The whole strategy behind disguising a bomb and hiding it in a public place is that people's curiosity (or perhaps simply their obliviousness) will cause them to get too close, causing instantaneous destruction to anyone within the blast range. In my years as a pastor (for that matter, in my years as a man) I have learned that there are time bombs in the realm of sexual intimacy. They look innocent enough and some of them don't always go off immediately. But sooner or later, unless they are warned, dating couples set one or more of them off, hurting themselves and often other innocent people around them.

It is my prayer that everyone who reads this book will develop a special relationship using the Dating Levels. As you progress through the bonding stages, you will protect one another by staying within the boundaries for each level. If you don't guard yourselves, you can be sure that one or more of the following "time bombs" will be your undoing.

TIME BOMB #1: LATE NIGHTS TALKING

Over the years, many couples have been in my office crying and hurting because they "just fell into having sex." It always seems to happen one night after talking until 2:00 in the morning. They say things like, "We just felt so close" (that is what intimate conversation will do) or, "We were so tired that we dropped our guard for a moment and then it was too late."

I cannot emphasize enough the need to impose a curfew if you want to stay within God's boundaries and develop the healthiest relationship possible. Even for the most relational people there is a saturation point where communication needs to cease. Your heart will generally run ahead of your mind, so prior to marriage, partake of intimate conversation in smaller bites so that your emotions do not get overwhelmed. The later the hour, the weaker your resistance will be to pressures on your moral standards. Say goodnight and go home, get into bed alone, and let God help you process your emotions after a good night's sleep.

TIME BOMB #2: INNOCENT COUCH CUDDLING

This time bomb often goes hand-in-hand with the first. This is an especially dangerous bomb for couples who are alone a lot and are at Level Three or Four. God has wired you so that the feeling of another person's body pressing against yours creates a powerful sensation that moves you toward greater levels of bonding. Couples act surprised that such an "innocent" thing could have exploded on them like that, but they shouldn't be. It is supposed to work that way.

If you light the fuse of a firecracker, it will explode because that's what it does. When you combine this cuddling with kissing it is like throwing gasoline on the fire; it will soon burn out of control. If you want to stay pure, my recommendation is that you not do this at all until you are married, or at least have others around whose presence will douse the flames.

TIME BOMB #3: JUST A BACK RUB

I know that you were only trying to serve them and meet a real need. I realize that they couldn't get an appointment with their chiropractor and they were in agony. But the power of touch was designed by God to stir strong physical and emotional reactions to encourage bonding. I'm not talking about a through-the-shirt, standing-up, with-others-around, five-minute back rub; I'm taking aim at the no-shirt, lying-down, we're-alone, extended back rub. If you allow yourself to get into this situation you need to know that statistically you are at great risk. Even if you don't progress into sexual touch and intercourse, most people become highly aroused in such situations. At the very least you are creating a lot of unnecessary sexual tension and frustration that you will have to deal with.

TIME BOMB #4: BELIEF THAT NO ACCOUNTABILITY IS NEEDED

The Bible says that pride comes before a fall and a truer word was never spoken. Volumes could be written about the need for accountability with a handful of trusted friends who have your best interest at heart and are not afraid to get in your face and ask the hard questions. I will not belabor this point other than to ask the following: why would you resist giving permission to friends to hold you accountable and help protect you from physical and sexual bonding that you know should be saved for marriage? Why would you resist letting them help protect you from something that can literally devastate a wonderful relationship—especially when relationships are so hard to find and develop?

TIME BOMB #5: SLEEPING OVER ON THE COUCH

"It was so late and he was so sleepy; driving home at that hour would have been dangerous." What were you doing staying up together so late? You know, a funny thing happens to the human mind when you are lying on a couch in the middle of the night and the person you feel so attracted to is only a few feet away in the bedroom. The range of rationalizations and the strength of sexual emotions grow exponentially in this situation. Doing this is the equivalent of sitting down next to a bomb, hugging it, and waiting for it to explode. I don't care if you couldn't hear any ticking or even if you have been trained to deal with time bombs; you are going to get hurt. The brave souls who defuse bombs for a living would tell you that they never underestimate a bomb, and they never play around with them. Maybe we should take their advice.

Three Kinds of Love

At Level Three, your knowledge of one another grows. If that knowledge creates greater appreciation and respect, you begin to have real feelings of love. This love should be a biblical love that covers all three aspects of love described in the Bible. While in English we have only the one word, in Greek, the language of the New Testament, there are several different words that describe the types of love we normally experience in dating, for our purposes here, I want to discuss the main three: *eros, philia,* and *agape.*

EROS: ROMANTIC LOVE

Let him kiss me with the kisses of his mouth—for your love is more delightful than wine. Pleasing is the fragrance of your perfumes; your name is like perfume poured out. No wonder the maidens love you! Take me away with you—let us hurry! Let the king bring me into his chambers. (Song of Solomon 1:2–4)

Eros is the love most people think about when they hear the word love in English. These are the emotional feelings of desire, appreciation, and attraction that stir a couple to move forward in the Bonding Stages.

PHILIA: FRIENDSHIP LOVE

But Timothy has just now come to us from you and has brought good news about your faith and love. He has told us that you always have pleasant memories of us and that you long to see us, just as we also long to see you...How can we thank God enough for you in return for all the joy we have in the presence of our God because of you? Night and day we pray most earnestly that we may see you again and supply what is lacking in your faith...May the Lord make your love increase and overflow for each other and for everyone else, just as ours does for you. (1 Thessalonians 3:6–12)

Clearly these verses are describing the warm feelings we have for good friends. These feelings of companionship, mutual trust, and strong affinity are what make friendships and marriages so much fun.

AGAPE: SACRIFICIAL LOVE

Love is patient, love is kind. It does not envy, it does not boast, it is not proud. It is not rude, it is not self-seeking, it is not easily angered, it keeps no record of wrongs. Love does not delight in evil but rejoices with the truth. It always protects, always trusts, always hopes, always perseveres. Love never fails. (1 Corinthians 13:4–8)

These familiar verses describe a special dimension of love that gives even if the other person doesn't give back in return. Loving like this is only possible when we receive love from God— the One who loved us even before we loved him. He is the only source of this kind of sacrificial love in the universe.

> The irony of Level Three is that you need to be careful to take your time just as things start to speed up and heat up.

Speaking of love, I recommend not saying, "I love you" until you are ready for a dozen roses and an engagement ring. Both of you must control your words and actions to avoid inappropriate bonding, and the man especially must be careful. Just as he cannot let his physical desires go beyond his commitment level, he also cannot carelessly use his words to manipulate a woman's emotions. Many unscrupulous men have used this phrase to deceive women into thinking they were bound for marriage. When pressed for sexual intimacy, a woman might concede "in the name of love," only to discover later that her "lover's" definition of love was actually lust. If you are following all of the instructions for these levels, you would be hard pressed to make such a foolish mistake.

If time and process confirm to you both that you have developed a true three-fold biblical love, then a major decision involving your Truth Triangles must take place. It will be time to decide whether or not you should get engaged. Chapter 14 is all about how to make such a decision. But the Truth Triangle still applies—at Level Three you've got to take your time and keep things in balance.

Even as you get closer to the person you are growing to love, you need to take plenty of time to reflect alone and pray. You also need to use a few trusted friends and family members as sounding boards. They will be able to give you honest and informed feedback because you have taken your time in this relationship and allowed friends and family many opportunities to get to know your partner. And when you let your friends and family be a part of the journey, they are better able to celebrate with you and give their blessing should you decide to move forward. The blessing of family and friends (assuming they are not highly dysfunctional) is an especially important piece of the puzzle. Without it, you greatly increase the risk of a failed or frustrating marriage.

The irony of Level Three is that you need to be careful to take your time just as things start to speed up and heat up. The next chapter will help you deal with this dilemma by explaining how to take your time and why you should.

Touchstones at Level Three

At Level Three, the rewards and the challenges are much greater. While the touchstones here are similar to those at Level Two, they go much deeper.

- **Don't ignore the spiritual component.** *Many couples at Level Three are so consumed with the emotions of their exclusive relationships that they ignore the spiritual component. Nothing could be worse. Actually, the volume should be turned up on the spiritual side of things. Each person should be drawing closer to God for the wisdom and power needed to navigate this wonderfully dangerous situation. You should want to see clear evidence that the other person owns their spiritual life. You should feel confident that they would continue walking with God, serving, having devotions, praying, and giving, even if you were no longer with them. If you can't trust them to follow God, how can you trust them on anything else?*
- **Spend ample time with family and close friends to allow feedback.** *Once the relationship gets to this point, it is easy to have blind spots and*

miss important details, both good and bad. Your family and friends can give you a perspective you don't have and really need—an objective one!

- **Continue the journey of conversation.** *While conversation is important at every level, it is especially important at Level Three. Too often couples get distracted with the kissing and touching and forget that the goal is a deep and intimate friendship. Talking in depth about personal plans, goals, values, priorities, and family is crucial. Notice I said personal plans and not joint plans. You need to hear what the other person desires and plans for their life even if you aren't with them. Shifting into making long-term plans as a couple must wait until you are engaged. Prior to that, such talk would imply a commitment that you haven't yet made. If you make most of your dates at this level one-on-one it will help provide time for such discussions. But remember, you still need to plan ample time with family and friends to keep an accurate perspective.*
- **Be exclusive.** *At Levels One and Two I have emphasized the casualness of the relationship, so I want to be sure I'm clear: at Level Three, you're not casual anymore. You're dating exclusively now. That is essential to protect and build trust that would be undermined if one member of the couple pursued others at Level One. Besides, why would you agree to be exclusive with someone and still keep your options open? That is not only immature but deceptive and selfish. I've seen many people do this only to ruin the good relationship they had.*
- **Protect your purity.** *If you are well suited and connecting emotionally and spiritually, you will generally feel an increase in sexual desire. If you go past the physical boundaries for this level you will truly regret it. Maintaining your purity is essential to putting the finishing touches on your mutual trust, which is one of the most important factors in successful marriages. This will require accountability with a few trusted friends—people who will ask the hard questions, pray for you, and exhort you to stay the course.*

CHAPTER THIRTEEN

Taking Your Time at Level Three

Dating Lie #13: Love at first sight is "real" love.

"Pastor Chuck, we're engaged, and we want you to marry us!" I sat across from this young couple in disbelief. She had been coming to our church for quite a while, but he had only shown up in the last couple of weeks. They had met at our singles event several days earlier (that's right—*days*) and had experienced an enormous degree of personal attraction. They had spent the entire night sitting in his car talking about everything from politics to deeply personal and vulnerable things. He had dropped her at her apartment at 3:30 a.m. and called her first thing when he woke up at 7:00 a.m. They talked on the way to work, met for lunch and dinner, and spent the rest of the evening driving through neighborhoods talking about what they wanted in a house. Long periods of passionate kissing and even more were sprinkled through that night and the next. Every day they talked in person or on the phone for hours, only stopping when sheer exhaustion forced them to go to bed.

By the sixth day, he proposed and they went to the mall to begin looking at rings. I still remember their anger when I informed them that I could not in good conscience perform their wedding. I offered instead to coach them through a process of backing way up in order to build a real relationship by going through the Dating Levels. As they left in a huff, they informed me that they would be finding another pastor at another church who would celebrate their good fortune with them. A few weeks later, they were married. A few months after that, they were separated and ultimately divorced. I honestly cannot remember the names of this man and woman, but I do remember the situation.

Over the years I have had this same conversation with multiple couples. Far too often the ending was tragic. But once in a while, a couple has had the maturity and self-control to listen to wisdom and slow down. These wiser couples spared themselves a lot of unnecessary pain. Sometimes their relationships ended at Level Two or Three, but they were able to keep their friendships intact. Other times, the couple would eventually get married, but only after going through the necessary stages that help make a strong relationship. Either way, the couples were thankful they listened to reason and learned the importance of three factors of influence: time, multiple environments, and controlled exposure.

Factor #1: Time

The amount, the frequency, and the quality of time you spend with someone have an enormous impact on the relationship. This is especially critical during the first two dating levels. Couples often spend way too many hours talking on the phone, instant messaging, texting, e-mailing or talking on a social networking site in addition to the time they talk on their official dates. This continuous interaction (sometimes late into the night) causes an unnaturally rapid progression to in-depth conversations about subjects that should be saved for Level Three and Level Four. Because a strong connection is made over such a short period of time, it gives a false sense of compatibility and even love. Such a connection has not undergone the testing and refining process of months of living life.

As Proverbs 19:2 says, "It is not good to have zeal without knowledge, nor to be hasty and miss the way." The rush of excitement you feel when you meet someone you are really attracted to is a powerful feeling. This verse reminds us that the zeal is great, but it is not based on much true knowledge about the person. As I said earlier, your feelings are *real*, but that doesn't mean they are *based in reality*. If you don't bring yourself under the control of the Holy Spirit, you will miss the way in your haste and potentially ruin a good thing.

The book of Proverbs has plenty to say about taking your time and not committing rashly. Proverbs 20:25 says, "It is a trap for a man to dedicate something rashly and only later to consider his vows."

> As Proverbs 19:2 says, "It is not good to have zeal without knowledge, nor to be hasty and miss the way." The rush of excitement you feel when you meet someone you are really attracted to is a powerful feeling. This verse reminds us that the zeal is great, but it is not based on much true knowledge about the person.

Slowing down externally is wise, but it is equally important that you slow down internally. The tendency is to make an internal commitment to the person because of the strong external feelings of attraction. This premature dedication of your heart can blind you to real problems later on because you will be internally determined to make it work no matter what. If time and interaction reveal that this person is "the one," you will have ample time to commit yourself completely, both internally and externally.

One last thing about time: remember that time apart is just as important as time together. Time apart allows your heart and mind to settle and regain balance. Your desires for greater commitment can be tested during these times to ensure that they are real and not overreactions. Also, you both need time to maintain your other friendships; because you will need those even if you do get married.

What are Good Time Boundaries for Levels One to Three?

Level One: *a call and date once or twice a month is more than sufficient.*

Level Two: *a weekly date and one to two contacts each week are appropriate.*

Level Three: *One to two dates and multiple calls per week would be a good balance of time.*

For the record, I recommend you date for at least one year before getting engaged. This allows ample time to experience all four seasons together and enough time at each level so that bonding is stable and healthy.

Factor #2: Multiple Environments

It is essential that you spend time together as a couple in multiple environments. You should be together at work functions, out on dates alone and with others, at family gatherings, and in community situations. You will learn a lot about a person as you observe him or her in these various environments. You will also learn a lot about your strengths and weaknesses as a couple. Ideally, you will compensate for one other's weaknesses and maximize one another's strengths. Social situations are ideal for discovering how to do this.

Another benefit is that you gain the educated input of family, friends, and coworkers who often notice things (good and bad) that you can't see. Not only does this help you stay balanced and clarify your feelings, but it also enables these same loved ones to be ready to support you should you get engaged or should the relationship end. If you haven't isolated yourself, it will be easy for your friends and family to provide the support you need if the relationship ends. If you get engaged and they have been able to give you positive feedback along the way, then they will be able to really celebrate with you when you share the news.

> If you haven't isolated yourself, it will be easy for your friends and family to provide the support you need if the relationship ends.

A few times I have seen couples who did not manage this factor and isolated themselves from family and friends. They moved very quickly into engagement and were upset at the lack of genuine excitement exhibited by their loved ones when the engagement was announced. This should make a clear point to the couple: the people who love them most and want what is best for them are naturally suspicious of anything they haven't been able to test over time. Don't make this mistake. The risk and cost are too great. Imagine if your child came home one day and announced he or she were getting married, and you hardly knew their partner. Wouldn't you have a hard time being excited?

Factor #3: Controlled Exposure

This factor involves the types of things you do at each dating level. Certain activities are more appropriate than others at each level and some remain high risk until after marriage. If you control the types of things you do together, then the feelings generated by your interactions will be consistent with the level of commitment you have made.

For example, at Level One, staying out really late talking about everything in your heart is not appropriate. It may seem romantic in the movies, but it creates strong feelings that are not based on experience and time. Fun activities like bowling, a movie, a company party, or a concert, are all very appropriate for this level. They help the couple have fun and allow any true attraction to manifest itself.

> Many couples have damaged and even broken a wonderful relationship because they dropped their guard this far into the game. It just isn't worth it!

At Level Two, kissing or talking about names for kids is out of bounds, as is looking at houses together. Instead, couples can stroll through the park talking about general life goals, participate in fun activities similar to those appropriate for Level One, or attend a Bible study together. These are exposures consistent with the commitment of this dating level.

At Level Three, any touching of anything that causes uncontrollable sexual tension is inappropriate. The couple should be especially careful not to fall prey to late nights, couch cuddling, sensuous back rubs, sleeping over, and no accountability. Many couples have damaged and even broken a wonderful relationship because they dropped their guard this far into the game. It just isn't worth it! A couple should not discuss issues that are typically reserved for premarital counseling such as budgets, sexual expectations, or time expectations. If you spend a lot of time sharing personal dreams, goals, values, and beliefs it will help you bond well. Consistent prayer and attending church together are also highly recommended. If you control the things you expose yourselves to, then you can properly build and protect your relationship.

Conclusion

As you wisely manage your time together, the environments you enter into, and the activities and situations to which you are exposed, you will begin to enjoy the fruits of your labor. Your diligence in these areas will provide the best soil for the bonding process to accomplish its work. The end result should be the following:

1. Healthy and appropriate intimacy.
2. Clarity about your feelings.
3. Knowledge of one another to give confidence about future decisions.
4. Familiarity with family and friendship issues—both good and bad.
5. Understanding and appreciation for your strengths and weaknesses.
6. Deeper love and respect for each other and for God.

As always, let me throw in the qualification that all this careful work on your relationship may reveal that the two of you are *not* suited for one another. When you have gained clarity about your feelings, you may be disappointed to learn that a relationship that seemed very promising at Level Two is not leading toward marriage. But that's a good thing. You have to trust the process and the God who uses the process to reveal his will in your life. If you have conducted yourself with integrity, you have nothing to fear.

It is possible, however, that Level Three dating will lead to Level Four. How will you make that judgment? Keep reading to find out.

How Do I Know If "This One" Is *"The* One"?

Dating Lie #14: You'll 'just know' when it's time to get married.

Over the years, I have had many men ask me a very pointed and passionate question: "How can I know for sure if she is the right one for me?" Typically this question is asked by a man who has been through Levels One and Two and has been dating a woman at Level Three for several months. He feels love for her, thinks they are well suited, and can't think of anything critical that they have not talked about. He often states that, while he feels love for her, he still notices attractive women and wonders if that means he doesn't love her enough. He knows he needs to make a decision about getting engaged. He knows that if he doesn't move forward, before long the relationship will likely have to end. He feels stuck, afraid, and anxious.

A wise person once said, "Begin with the end in mind." Unless you have a clear goal you may not like the results produced by your efforts and time. Applied to dating, it would sound something like this, "Begin dating with a clear understanding of how you will date and what kind of person you want to end up with."

I know that the hopeless romantics out there are already jumping out of their seats in protest, but the undeniable reality is that we all have criteria we use to decide who's dateworthy. We have even more specific ideas about the kind of person we would marry. The problem is that these criteria are, for the most part, under the surface of our consciousness; they shape our responses without our giving them much thought. I believe that God has given us guidance about the general criteria we should look for when dating or considering marriage. The specific criteria are typically more in the realm of the mystery of attraction, and since I believe that is unique for everyone, I will not attempt to deal with that further.

I want to provide you with two things. First, I want to give you general biblical criteria to help you choose people to date. Second, I want to give you a list of assessment questions that will help you determine whether or not you should move up to Level Four. I have had the privilege of talking with hundreds of singles and guiding them through the process of determining if they should move to the next level of commitment. From these experiences and from the parameters of the Dating Levels, I believe I can give you some very helpful questions to aid in your decision making.

Spiritual Compatibility

Do not be yoked together with unbelievers. For what do righteousness and wickedness have in common? Or what fellowship can light have with darkness? What harmony is there between Christ and Belial? What does a believer have in common with an unbeliever? What agreement is there between the temple of God and idols? For we are the temple of the living God. (2 Corinthians 6:14–16)

Amazingly enough, spiritual compatibility is often the last issue considered, and sometimes it is not considered at all. People live out of their philosophy of life. That means spiritual compatibility is issue number one. All major decisions about values, right and wrong, and family issues flow out of a person's spiritual perspective. Even atheists live out of a philosophy of life. The problem is that they are their own standard of right and wrong, so you either agree with them, or you are wrong. For an atheist, there is no Bible to appeal to for clarity and unity of agreement. It is an unstable foundation for life and marriage.

> The biblical mandate to sacrificially love one another creates a stronger likelihood that a disagreement can be resolved in a healthy and unified way.

Christians, on the other hand have a great advantage. Believers have strong opinions just like everyone else, but the difference is that two believers can disagree and then go to the Bible for clarity. Whatever the Bible says on the issue they both must accept and alter their own opinions. On issues that the Bible doesn't address (e.g. should we buy this house or not), there is often general advice related to the topic. But even when there isn't, the biblical mandate to sacrificially love one another creates a stronger likelihood that a disagreement can be resolved in a healthy and unified way. Beyond the decision-making problem there is also the issue of four-fold bonding—physically, mentally, emotionally, and spiritually. If you are spiritually incompatible, you will be limited to three quarters of the intimacy God intended for you. Your spiritual life is the most important part of you; going in different directions spiritually will negatively affect your physical, emotional, and mental intimacy with your partner.

Some people believe in what is called "missionary dating." The idea is that by dating someone of another faith (or no faith at all) you will influence them to receive Christ. I need to give a strong caution here. The bonding process works whether you are a believer or not. It is God's design for all humans. If you spend enough time with someone, you will begin bonding. Left unchecked, you could find yourself at the point of either marrying someone who doesn't share your faith and parameters of truth for decision making (a recipe for a volatile marriage), or you will feel compelled to end a year-long relationship that never should have started.

> Your spiritual life is the most important part of you; going in different directions spiritually will negatively affect your physical, emotional, and mental intimacy with your partner.

Noble Character

A wife of noble character who can find? She is worth far more than rubies. Her husband has full confidence in her and lacks nothing of value. She brings him good, not harm, all the days of her life. She selects wool and flax and works with eager hands. She is like the merchant ships, bringing her food from afar. She gets up while it is still dark; she provides food for her family and portions for her servant girls. She considers a field and buys it; out of her earnings she plants a vineyard. She sets about her work vigorously; her arms are strong for her tasks. She sees that her trading is profitable, and her lamp does not go out at night. In her hand she holds the distaff and grasps the spindle with her fingers. She opens her arms to the poor and extends her hands to the needy. When it snows, she has no fear for her household; for all of them are clothed in scarlet. She makes coverings for her bed; she is clothed in fine linen and purple. Her husband is respected at the city gate, where he takes his seat among the elders of the land. (Proverbs 31:10–23)

The passage is talking specifically about wives, but the same is true for husbands. You want a spouse who exhibits noble character.

The beauty of the Dating Levels is that it has a built-in process of time, multiple environments, and controlled exposure that allows you to learn and test a person's character. If you don't see clear evidence of noble character on the first date, you may want to seriously consider whether or not it is wise to go out with them again. If, at Level Three, you have reason to suspect the nobleness of the other person's character, that is not something you should ignore.

Availability

You shall not commit adultery...You shall not covet your neighbor's wife, or his manservant or maidservant, his ox or donkey, or anything that belongs to your neighbor. (Exodus 20:14,17)

Unfortunately today, I have to take the time to state what should be obvious: Don't be a home wrecker. While most people agree with this in principle, too many in our culture think they are the exception to the rule. I emphatically say, "No, you're not!" A person who is married is not biblically available to you, no matter how strong the attraction. A person who is separated is not biblically available to you, no matter what the legal definitions say. A person who is recently divorced should not be quickly entering a new relationship. The rule of thumb for reasonable healing time is no less than one year and often three or more years to process through the grief and anger. There is also a need to sort through the personal attraction grid issues that attracted them to a person who would abandon them or be unfaithful. A national ministry called Divorce Care is an excellent resource for healing the trauma of divorce for adults and for children who are affected.

If you don't see clear evidence of noble character on the first date, you may want to seriously consider whether or not it is wise to go out with them again.

Moving Forward

At the end of each section, I've offered a few questions to help you decide whether or not it is time to move to the subsequent level. But you have to admit, moving from Level Three to Level Four is a whole different thing. Accordingly, I have provided below a much lengthier and more specific list of questions to help you assess whether or not it is right to take that giant step forward. Consider all of the following questions seriously and pray through them before moving to Level Four.

1. How have you grown spiritually, individually and as a couple, at Level Three?
2. How strong is your attraction to this person (compared with your attraction at Levels One and Two):
   a. Spiritually
   b. Mentally
   c. Emotionally
   d. Physically

3. Is your Truth Triangle in balance?

4. Does this person have any explosive emotional issues such as anger, jealousy, manic depression, addiction, narcissism, or unhealthy parental attachments?

5. Does this person have any unresolved conflicts such as a former spouse and/or children, legal loose ends, or issues from being abused?

6. How are you similar and how are you different? Is this okay with you?

7. Would your friends be surprised or concerned by your engagement?

8. Would your family be surprised or concerned by your engagement?

9. Have you been maintaining sexual purity? If not, is this distorting your perception?

10. Does this person handle money well? Are they in a lot of debt? Do they tithe?

11. Does this person manage time in a way that is acceptable to you?

12. Does this person have any annoying habits that you hope will change after marriage?

13. Does this person have a history of keeping promises?

14. Is this person often negative or critical about life or you?

15. Do others think this person is somewhat controlling?

16. Can you express your honest feelings to this person without fear? Do you feel heard and see evidence that your opinions are valued?

17. How well have you handled conflict with each other in the past?

18. Do you see regular evidence that this person has his or her own personal and vibrant relationship with Jesus Christ that will not go away even if you break-up?

19. Have you gone through a tough time together such as a job loss or death of a loved one? Did you function well as a team and feel supported and able to support?

20. As a couple, do you talk too little, too much, or just enough for your needs?

21. Do you anticipate any challenges with specific family members at marriage?

22. Do you like doing a lot of the same things? Is there any activity in which your partner participates that you are uncomfortable with?

23. Do you like how your partner's parents treat one another?

24. Have you seen your partner interact with children? Is it acceptable to you? Have you discussed having children and do you agree about it?

25. Are you confident from previous experience that your partner will choose you over a family member, even a parent?

26. Have you made any decisions together and did you feel good about it?

27. Are you and your partner able to not be together on a regular basis so that you have personal time and time with friends? Has there been any conflict in this area?

28. Do you and your partner have agreement about your roles as husband and wife?

These questions should help both of you see more clearly whether or not you are ready and willing to be married to the other. The ritual of the man asking you to marry him is important. But if the two of you have followed the process, the decision will have already been made in your hearts before that wonderful moment.

Here's one final comment specifically for men that may seem minor, but really isn't: I strongly recommend that you put a lot of thought into how you will ask her to marry you. The entire event from start to finish will be something you both remember forever. It is especially important to her for reasons you will never quite understand. Multitudes of people over the years will ask her to recount the story. Give her something really good to share.

Dating and Engaged to You

They say marriages are made in heaven, but so are thunder and lightning.

—Clint Eastwood[11]

I remember the night my wife and I got engaged. It was Valentine's Day, and I had made reservations at a very nice restaurant. We ordered our food, and then the roses arrived. I had arranged for a dozen red roses to be delivered to our table. As she smelled the flowers and sat back to take in their beauty, I pulled a card out of my pocket. In the card I proclaimed my love for her and asked if she would look up and tell me she would be my wife. She paused for what seemed an eternity. Panic welled up inside of me as I wondered if she had had a change of heart and was thinking of a polite way to say no. (She later said she was simply savoring the moment.) As she looked up and said yes, I handed her the ring box. I moved to her side of the table, and for the rest of the evening, we sat in a wonderful fog, talking about the future and letting our very expensive steak and lobster get cold. I don't think either one of us ate more than a few bites.

Later, as we walked around her neighborhood, we stopped at a spot where the two of us had sat several months earlier. We had been in an exclusive relationship for a while, and on that night, I asked her if she was willing to continue, knowing that I was in the ministry and might be led by God to go to distant lands. Before I risked allowing greater feelings to develop between us, I needed to know if she trusted God enough to trust what he might do with me. She told me that, while she might be scared at first, if God meant us to be together, she would go wherever he led us. On our engagement night, we paused at that spot, remembered, and kissed. It was a special moment. Up to that point we had learned a lot about each other, but there was still much more to learn. That is why Level Four dating is so important.

CHAPTER FIFTEEN

Defining Level Four

Dating Lie #15: We're engaged so sex is okay.

Level Four dating takes place during the engagement period. This is a joyous time, but it is also an extremely stressful time, especially for the bride to be. This is one of the toughest levels to handle because you begin to feel many of the pressures of married life without all the benefits. Planning a wedding can take on a life of its own, so the relational side of things must be guarded and nurtured.

To the Mall Again

For a year or more, you have returned to the relational mall week after week learning the ins and outs of the first three levels and daring to go up escalator after escalator until you reached the fourth level—engagement. At the top of the escalator you take the first step of engagement and enter the jewelry store. Stepping out of the jewelry store, you gaze upstairs to the fifth and final level. There you see businesses like the bank, Victoria's Secret, and the maternity shop.

As you stroll through this fourth level of the mall, the ring feels wonderfully unusual on your finger.[12] You find yourself fiddling with it when your mind is preoccupied. As he draws you close with his arm around your waist, you put your head on his shoulder and your hand on his chest. The ring catches the lights overhead and flashes brilliant colors of promise for the years ahead.

You go into the tuxedo store to decide what the groom and groomsmen should wear. The choices are limitless, but you have always envisioned a particular style and look, which you point out in the book. You have thought about the details of your wedding your whole life, but he has only thought about getting married. Details of this nature went right past him for the most part. As long as your ideas are not too extreme, he generally feels fine about them. The first of many tense moments begins, however, when you start discussing the cost of things. The differences between men and women begin to be more evident as perspectives on values collide at a new level. The lessons of communication and interaction learned over the last year or so provide the resources and the wisdom to navigate successfully through such disagreements.

After leaving the tuxedo store, you pass the bridal shop. You ask him to pray for you because in two weeks you will be meeting your mother in that store to pick out a wedding gown. And one week later, you will be there with your girlfriends to pick out bridesmaids dresses. After all, these are wonderful events, but they are also times that can be relationally tricky. Feelings can be hurt and frustrations can flourish. You will need God's wisdom and Spirit to balance your desires with accommodating the needs of others.

Next, you go into the department store to complete the bridal registry. This is a new experience for him. Up to this point, the only time he has ever been in this part of the store is when he accompanied you to buy a gift for friends who were getting married. The two of you spend hours debating about china, silverware, colors of the bathroom, kitchen appliances, and countless other things you place on the list and hope to receive as wedding gifts. He comments how complicated this is getting and how he feels his vote is not as important as yours. Now would be a good time to stop and remember that a wedding is an event, but a marriage is a lifetime. You make amends and commit yourselves to balancing the demands of the wedding event with the delights of the lifelong relationship. A hug, a kiss, and a prayer help to patch things up. You finish your registry and head off to the restaurant for a romantic dinner—and perhaps some discussion about who should be invited to the wedding.

After you leave the mall, the two of you go back to your house to continue the discussion about the invitation list. An hour later, you share coffee and a time of cuddling on the couch. It feels so good and right to be there. Your desires, which have been slowly awakened and stirred over the last year, suddenly flare up with an urgency you haven't previously experienced. The kissing leads to lying down on the couch and drawing each other close. Your mind is reeling, but your heart is rejoicing. After all the hard work and stress of planning, a little emotional and physical reward seems justified. But a year's worth of balancing your Truth Triangles and praying together has created a storehouse of self-control and responsibility. You both know that to go any further would seriously undermine the trust in your marriage.

The point of this self-control, by the way, isn't just obedience, though that would be reason enough. Self-control now means better sex later. The world's advice is that you should drive a car before you buy it; therefore sex before marriage is the wise thing to do. But in his book *Men and Marriage*, sociologist George Gilder cites statistics showing that men who fulfill their sexual desires prior to marriage have significantly higher rates of suicide, drug and alcohol addiction, mental disease, accidental death, and arrest.[13] More and more the wisdom of God's Word starts to make sense.

Back to Our Couple on the Couch

Even though your immediate sexual desires want to agree with everything you've always heard in the world, deep down you know it isn't true. So, with strength drawn from the indwelling Spirit of God, you stop, sit up, and bring yourselves under control. You sit at the table and talk about the need to limit the amount of kissing and intimate hugging you do between now and the wedding.

This is what I call the "holy pause." You may have noticed in the chart in Chapter 1 that you move from bonding stage to bonding stage in every other dating level. But at Level Four, you stay put. You shouldn't move into any new bonding stages until you marry (at which time you'll be bursting through them with joyful abandon). It's possible that the wise thing is to take a step back and have less physical contact. You'll need to talk about that, of course, communicating that this backing off is not a sign of rejection but one of respect, love, and protection. You've waited this long, a few more months won't kill you—it just feels like it will.

You agree that it's time for your fiancé to go home. He gives you a safe hug and kiss, and before he heads for the door, you pray together and thank God for helping you wait, committing yourselves to protecting one another and saving your passion for the honeymoon. Before you go to sleep, you thank God for having a fiancé who feels such passion for you, but who cares more about you than he cares about himself—what a blessing!

You pass the next few months attending wedding showers, dinner parties, and squeezing in some private talks and walks whenever possible. Occasionally, you question the wisdom of not eloping and sparing yourselves all this stress. But you know that you will be forever glad that you had a wedding like this.

You find yourselves at Home Depot picking out items for the house or apartment that you will soon share together. More of the adjustments of two becoming one are felt as you have to compromise on what you like and want.

It's possible that the wise thing is to take a step back and have less physical contact. You'll need to talk about that, of course, communicating that this backing off is not a sign of rejection but one of respect, love, and protection. You've waited this long, a few more months won't kill you—it just feels like it will.

To be sure you have adequately thought through all of the relevant issues, I highly recommend premarital counseling. In addition, the evaluation tool *Prepare/Enrich* is an excellent resource to help you prepare for the challenges ahead.[14] The evaluation focuses on ten major issues that you will discuss with your counselor or pastor:

1. **Personality Issues:** This addresses temperament differences and how they can affect your relationship.
2. **Communication:** Areas where communication will be difficult are discussed and coping strategies are devised.
3. **Conflict Resolution:** By identifying any areas of strong divergence, the tool helps couples be prepared for conflicts in certain areas. Skills to handle them are also provided.
4. **Financial Management:** *It is vital to* create a budget and discuss values and priorities regarding debt, savings, and lending money.
5. **Leisure Activities:** Every couple experiences stress due to different energy levels and personal preferences.

Making agreements about how much time is spent alone and with others is wise.

6. **Sexual Relationship:** Much discussion needs to happen here regarding expectations, fears, taboos, basic knowledge of anatomy, and biblical perspectives to help you have a vibrant and fulfilling sex life.

7. **Children and Parenting:** Clarity about expectations and desires for having children and child rearing need to be reached to avoid undue stress.

8. **Family and Friends:** Clarity about setting boundaries for family and friends is important, as is mutual agreement in terms of how much time, money, and energy will be invested in these relationships.

9. **Equalitarian Roles:** Who does what in and around the home is a major source of contention. Even more explosive can be the control issues that surface when discussing how and when things are to get done. This also explores biblical perspectives on decision making, especially when the two of you disagree.

10. **Religious Orientation:** Many people underestimate the importance and impact this has on a marriage. It typically becomes a major issue when children are born or in times of crisis, but it also dramatically affects daily life. For instance, the Christian belief that we are to lay down our lives for one another and love sacrificially can make daily life much less combative, especially if both husband and wife practice this under the power of the Holy Spirit. But what happens if one or both are more hedonistic in their philosophy and want everything their way?

As you go through premarital counseling together, you begin to clarify agreements and expectations on things like time, money, children, family boundaries, roles and responsibilities, and even sexual intimacy. It seems like a lot to take in, and it becomes obvious that a few issues will cause more angst later on than others. But you have been able to achieve a reasonable agreement and understanding on each issue, so you have even more confidence and peace about saying, "I do."

Conclusion

Level Four is about preparation and clarification. A great deal of time and energy is put into preparing for the wedding day and beginning life together. The stress levels increase dramatically, as do the expectations of family and friends from both sides. An equal amount of time and energy should be spent on clarification and agreement about expectations and boundaries regarding issues like money, time, family, roles, and sex. Premarital counseling is highly recommended and tools such as *Prepare/Enrich* are excellent resources.

A pastor or professional Christian counselor can make a world of difference in how easily you make the transition into married life, especially the adjustments typical in the first year. So during this level, all of your energy is spent on getting ready to be married. It won't be much longer until the big day arrives!

Touchstones at Level Four:

Pay attention to the following things at Level Four:
- ***Stay focused in the midst of wedding planning.*** *Far too often I have seen couples drift apart because they are consumed by the enormous number of details that a wedding requires. Add to that the stress caused by planning and everyone is too tired to do anything but sleep or cuddle. By now you can see what a negative direction that is. If you aren't careful, you could find yourself enjoying a well-planned wedding while trying to remember why you wanted to get married. You can also accumulate a lot of unresolved wounds from the fast-paced interaction of the engagement. These wounds are generally not mortal wounds, but*

they will come forth as soon as you have time and space for them to surface—the honeymoon. You must make time during the engagement to
nourish and build your relationship by talking and praying about things
other than the wedding.

- **Honor the "holy pause."** It is so easy to slip here. You feel committed, you feel love, you feel desire, and you have waited so long—that is
precisely my point. You've waited this long, a few more months will not
kill you, but violating your conscience and God's design could kill your
relationship. Don't enter the three bonding stages that are reserved for
marriage. Stand fast, pray, and even back off some of the acceptable levels of physical contact for a while if that is what it takes to protect each
other's purity. You are a team; work together!

- **Prepare to redefine family boundaries.** As you become husband and
wife, the leaving and cleaving commanded in Scripture must take place.
That means that your spouse to be is now more important than your
mother, your father, or any friend. This will cause some natural tension.
Your parents know this needs to happen, but rarely are they prepared for
it. The same angst they felt when you went off to kindergarten, then to
college, and later moved into your own apartment will well up in their
hearts. These feelings will pass if the parent has a healthy understanding of God's Word and a good relationship with him. If not, you will need
to be prepared to do some gentle but firm teaching by speaking the truth
in love so that they will know where you stand. You will also need to
make sure you and your spouse are on the same page and will not allow
a family member, friend, or child to divide you. You are two, but you
need to start thinking and acting as one.

- **Premarital counseling.** Many couples make the costly mistake of
thinking that they already have clarity and agreement about all issues.
Even those couples who dated well and spent a year or two together
before engagement, still need a knowledgeable person to guide them
through some key issues. In my counseling over the years, I have found
that I can get even the healthiest couples to argue in less than ten minutes by asking certain questions. The point is not to make them argue,
but to help them see that they are only beginning their journey. The experience of others can help them avoid a lot of unnecessary fights so that
they can save their energy for solving inevitable difficulties.

CHAPTER SIXTEEN

Resolving Conflict

Dating Lie #16: We're perfect for each other
because we never argue.

Some relationships don't involve any conflict at all. You probably know people with whom you've never had a disagreement. But you probably don't know those people very well. The truth of the matter is that any relationship with any depth will involve conflict. You could ignore the conflict, but that's not the same thing as being free from conflict. It's not healthy either. If you want to have healthy relationships, you have to know how to handle conflict.

A lot of couples are alarmed to realize that they have more conflict after they get engaged. There are a few reasons for that. One is that there is simply more to disagree about when you're engaged. You're making many decisions, and you can't possibly agree on every one. Another reason is that you're spending a lot more time together. Again, more time together means more opportunities for conflict. But a third reason—one you should not ignore—is simply this: when you are fully committed to another person you naturally feel freer to express your true feelings, both good and bad. When you feel the possibility that the other person might go away, you might feel the need to hide your true feelings lest you run them off. Sometimes it's a good sign—a sign of greater security and comfort—when you loosen up and have a few arguments.

Below are some tips for resolving the most common conflicts that will arise in your relationships. These tips apply to any relationship, at any level. I include them here in the Level Four section as a way of highlighting the fact that if you don't get your conflict resolution skills in shape while you're engaged, your marriage will suffer.

> A lot of couples are alarmed to realize that they have more conflict after they get engaged.

Blame Shifting

Blame shifting was one of the very first relational tricks men and women ever learned, and it didn't work out very well. Remember when God called Adam and Eve to account for eating the forbidden fruit in the Garden of Eden? Adam said, "'The woman you put here with me, she gave me some fruit from the tree, and I ate it'" (Genesis 3:12). Real nice—blame the woman. Actually, Adam did worse than that. He blamed God—"the woman *you* put here with me." Eve did a little better: "'The serpent deceived me, and I ate'" (Genesis 3:13). True enough. But she still wasn't taking responsibility for her actions.

One of the most frustrating things for a pastor is counseling with couples who are blame shifting. If you've ever played Whac-A-Mole at the state fair, then you have a good mental image of what this is like. First she says he did something; then he counters with what she did, and the game is on. No matter what the counselor says, the fighting won't stop because they each want to be right, and neither is willing to accept any responsibility. As long as they maintain this attitude, no resolution can be found.

Easy Anger and Reckless Words

A fool shows his annoyance at once, but a prudent man overlooks an insult. A truthful witness gives honest testimony, but a false witness tells lies. Reckless words pierce like a sword, but the tongue of the wise brings healing. (Proverbs 12:16–18)

I must confess that this is one of my personal struggles. God is still working on my soul to heal my short fuse (which is another way of saying selfishness). Temperament plays into this, but when all is said and done, each person is responsible to maintain an approachable and reasonable demeanor. Impatience and taking offense are evidence of our sinful nature. I just have to own my sin of being easily frustrated and angered.

My wife would tell you that she struggles with reckless words. As a kid she learned to defend herself with a sharp tongue. After we were married, I was the victim of her skill many times. She perceived me as strong and tough and thought her words couldn't hurt me. Because of this she was less careful when she was hurt or angry with me. The truth is that she is actually the only person who can truly hurt me with words because she is my wife and soul mate. "The wise woman builds her house, but with her own hands the foolish one tears hers down" (Proverbs 14:1). This verse is so powerful it bears reading slowly and out loud. You either build or destroy with your words.

Pride and Arrogance

A wise son heeds his father's instruction, but a mocker does not listen to rebuke. From the fruit of his lips a man enjoys good things, but the unfaithful have a craving for violence. He who guards his lips guards his life, but he who speaks rashly will come to ruin...Pride only breeds quarrels, but wisdom is found in those who take advice. (Proverbs 13:1–3, 10)

Another common communication killer is pride and arrogance. Many people have developed the bad habit of tearing other people down. When they are confronted, they say they are just joking but everyone knows better. Putting others down and mocking another person's ideas and opinions not only kills intimacy but also proves you have a pride problem. Another manifestation of this is interrupting the other person and giving your answer before he or she has finished speaking.

> Putting others down and mocking another person's ideas and opinions not only kills intimacy but also proves you have a pride problem.

As one who processes thoughts quickly and likes to be right, I can attest to the negative impact this has on relationships. This nasty habit must be seen as the enemy. You must unlearn this habit and replace it with a humble and listening ear.

Argument Escalation

"A gentle answer turns away wrath, but a harsh word stirs up anger" (Proverbs 15:1).

One of the hardest skills to learn is how to keep from escalating an argument. If you can remember that the other person is not under the control of the Holy Spirit when he or she is speaking harsh and attacking words, it will help you to see that person as a victim of enemy attack. In these moments, pray that both of you would recognize the enemy's hand and begin hearing the voice of God instead.

The Habitually Angry Partner

> Warn a divisive person once, and then warn him a second time. After that, have nothing to do with him. You may be sure that such a man is warped and sinful; he is self-condemned. (Titus 3:10-11)

There are some people with whom you simply cannot resolve conflict. They have issues that have nothing to do with you, and until they deal with those issues themselves, you won't be able to make peace with them. Sometimes you have to put a boundary of separation between yourself and a habitually negative person in order to stay healthy. If the person is someone you are dating, then it should be obvious that the relationship is not healthy and should come to an end.

Conflict Resolution in Five Steps

1. Select one topic at a time to discuss

   Don't jump to a new topic until the first one is resolved. One of the most unproductive things couples do is try to resolve conflict inside of a pinball machine. Neither person can truly hear the other or process the facts and emotions when more and more issues keep being bounced onto the table.

2. Separate facts from feelings

   One of the biggest mistakes couples make is to use 'all or nothing' language. Statements such as "you always" or "you never" paint the other person's behavior in absolute terms which will definitely be resisted by them and put them on the defensive. Instead, couples should use phrases such as, "I FEEL like you frequently do that irritating thing." Comments like this are much easier to hear and more accurate.

3. Separate friend from foe

   Remember, your partner is not the enemy, but Satan truly is! As I've stated before, you must see your partner as your friend. He or she may be a very frustrating or callous friend at that moment, but a friend nevertheless. Restating your commitments to one another before, during, and after a conflict is very wise. Often after my wife and I have had a disagreement, I will tell her, "I still love you and I'm still glad I married you. Nothing can change that!" It may sound a little awkward or corny in the moment, but I think it helps heal our hearts.

4. Seek a win/win/win

   Solutions must be good for you, your partner, and for God. Conflict resolution is not like the game Capture the Flag. The winner is not the one who conquers all the other players. In a relationship, most conflict is about preferences, opinions, and misunderstanding, and with these types of issues there is plenty of room for everyone to win. Obviously, for the times when the conflict is about real sin, there is a right and wrong position, though the truth still needs to be spoken in love.

5. Schedule maintenance

   Regular date nights provide ample time for talking, which can head off conflicts before they spring up. This is especially important after marriage, when life gets very full very fast. Sometimes, setting an appointment with each other to have tough conversations is a wise strategy. If a discussion is going badly, it is often a good idea to call a time-out and set a time to reconvene once everyone's emotions have been brought under the control of the Holy Spirit. In the downtime while you're waiting for the next conversation, I recommend you pray for the other person and listen to God. It is usually easier to hear I'm wrong from God than my spouse. Often the Lord will show me that I'm wrong, so I can go to my wife, confess, and ask forgiveness. Other times, he makes it clear that I am right and she is wrong, and at those times he always moves me to pray for her. It is easier for her to hear it from him also, so praying is always a good thing to do.

Restating your commitments to one another before, during, and after a conflict is very wise.

By practicing this conflict resolution method you will develop the skills necessary to work through almost anything with anyone. It will help you move to higher dating levels, and if you get married, it will enable you and your spouse to live with a degree of harmony and cooperation that most people only dream about.

CHAPTER SEVENTEEN
Let's Talk about Sex

Dating Lie #17: Sex is like hunger: you have to feed it.

Sometimes the best way to deal with temptation is to rule it out in advance. According to Harry Truman's biographer, David McCullough, President Truman was under incredible pressure while attending the Potsdam Conference. One evening, near the end of an arduous session, Truman prepared to leave for his nearby lodgings. A young Army public relations officer, seeing Truman about to leave, stuck his head in the window of his car and asked to hitch a ride. Truman told him to get in and the two struck up a conversation that was overheard and later reported by Truman's driver.

There's no way around it; you are going to have sexual energy and especially when you are engaged.

In Berlin the black market was rampant, and everything was available—cigarettes, watches, whiskey, and prostitutes. The officer said that if there was anything the President wanted, anything at all he needed, he had only to say the word. "Anything, you know, like women." Truman bristled. "Listen, son, I married my sweetheart," he said. "She doesn't run around on me, and I don't run around on her. I want that understood.

Don't ever mention that kind of stuff to me again." Truman's driver later recalled, "By the time we were home, he got out of the car and never even said goodbye to that guy."[15]

If you are human, you regularly face this issue of how to appropriately deal with your God-given sexual energy. God created hormones, the male and female genders, the body parts necessary for sex, the wiring in our brains that stimulate our desires for sex and sexual response, and he created the institution of marriage. In the Bible, God does not shy away from dealing with this topic in a clear and forthright manner.

> The God who created sex wants his married children to enjoy it with passion and abandon.

There's no way around it; you are going to have sexual energy and especially when you are engaged. In order to learn how to handle your sexual energy, there are five things you need to understand: the general principles of sexuality, the two options for releasing sexual energy, the divine design of the sexual systems, the reality of sexual time bombs, and biblical answers to sexual questions.

Understanding the General Principles of Sexuality

PRINCIPLE #1: GOD IS IN FAVOR OF SEX

As I mentioned at Level Two, God is not a prude; he is prudent. He created sex, and he knows that sexual intimacy can only be a blessing in the context of marriage. "Marriage should be honored by all, and the marriage bed kept pure, for God will judge the adulterer and all the sexually immoral" (Hebrews 13:4).

The God who created sex wants his married children to enjoy it with passion and abandon. If you don't believe it, just read this passage from the Song of Solomon:

"Let him kiss me with the kisses of his mouth—for your love is more delightful than wine....

Take me away with you—let us hurry! Let the king bring me into his chambers." (Song of Solomon 1:2, 4)

The writer of the Song of Solomon was writing under the inspiration of the Holy Spirit just like all the authors of the books of the Bible. It has a racy tone because God wants married couples to enjoy passion. He's not embarrassed to talk about it, so we shouldn't be either.

PRINCIPLE #2: GOD INTENDED SEX TO TAKE PLACE BETWEEN A MAN AND A WOMAN

Despite present cultural proclamations, heterosexuality has always been the plan. "So God created man in his own image, in the image of God he created him; male and female he created them" (Genesis 1:27). Romans 1 is even more specific and makes it clear that homosexuality is a distortion of God's design.

Because of this, God gave them over to shameful lusts. Even their women exchanged natural relations for unnatural ones. In the same way the men also abandoned natural relations with women and were inflamed with lust for one another. Men committed indecent acts with other men, and received in themselves the due penalty for their perversion. (Romans 1:26–27)

I know it is not popular to speak about homosexuality this way, but it's what the Bible clearly teaches in multiple places. God intended sex to be between a man and a woman who are married to each other. There is something about the male and female image coming together as one that reveals the character of God in a way that nothing else on earth can. Also, this marriage picture is proclaimed to be symbolic of Jesus' commitment to the church on earth. It is important to God that this image be preserved.

> Any cursory reading on the causes of sexual addiction and pornography will confirm that the problem is not a lack of sex, but a lack of intimacy, which loosely defined is human interaction based in love and respect.

PRINCIPLE #3: SEX IS WONDERFUL, BUT NOT NECESSARY FOR OUR SURVIVAL

Again, despite present cultural proclamations, you will not die if you don't have sex or sexual release. Sexual desire is not like hunger or thirst. If you don't eat food or drink water you will eventually die. This is not true for sex. Millions of people every day live normal and healthy lives without sexual intimacy. Beyond food, water, and shelter, the only thing people need for survival is some sort of human contact and support such as non-sexual touch and conversation. Any cursory reading on the causes of sexual addiction and pornography will confirm that the problem is not a lack of sex, but a lack of intimacy, which loosely defined is human interaction based in love and respect. Severe isolation leads ultimately to mental and emotional instability, but not having sex does not have such serious consequences. While it is an important part of a healthy marriage, when health or other factors make it impossible, couples who regularly connect in the other bonding stages continue to flourish.

You Can Control Your Sexual Desires

> It is *God's will that you should be sanctified*: that you should
> avoid sexual immorality; that *each of you should learn to
> control his own body* in a way that is holy and honorable,
> not in passionate lust like the heathen, who do not know
> God; and that in this matter no one should wrong his
> brother or take advantage of him. The Lord will punish
> men for all such sins, as we have already told you and
> warned you. *For God did not call us to be impure, but to live
> a holy life.* Therefore, he who rejects this instruction does
> not reject man but God, who gives you his Holy Spirit.
> (1 Thessalonians 4:3–8, emphasis added)

Most of my life I have heard people proclaim that you cannot
control your sexual desire, arguing that we are just animals
acting on instinct. According to God that is just not true. Not
only can we learn to "control our own bodies," but it is God's
will that we do so. He will help us via the power of his Holy Spirit
indwelling us if we will let him. There are two main options for
controlling our sexual energy and desires that God provides.

Understanding the Two Options for Releasing Sexual Energy

OPTION #1: THE WEDDING OPTION

> May your fountain be blessed, and may you rejoice in
> the wife of your youth.
>   A loving doe, a graceful deer— may her breasts sat-
> isfy you always, may you ever be captivated by her love.
> Why be captivated, my son, by an adulteress?
>   Why embrace the bosom of another man's wife?
> (Proverbs 5:18–20)

The wedding option is the only option that allows you to actually have sex. By following God's relational design, moving step by step through the Dating Levels and Bonding Stages you come to the place of making a permanent, official, and public commitment to your partner. This creates a protected bond and makes healthy intimate sexual expression possible. This union is not merely allowed by God, but he blesses it as well. In this option, your sexual energy is released in an act of love with your spouse.

> Not only can we learn to "control our own bodies," but it is God's will that we do so.

OPTION #2: THE SERVICE OPTION

> My command is this: Love each other as I have loved you. Greater love has no one than this, that he lay down his life for his friends. You are my friends if you do what I command. I no longer call you servants, because a servant does not know his master's business. Instead, I have called you friends, for everything that I learned from my Father I have made known to you. You did not choose me, but I chose you and appointed you to go and bear fruit—fruit that will last. Then the Father will give you whatever you ask in my name. This is my command: Love each other. (John 15:12–17)

The service option requires you to take all of your sexual energy and re-channel it into living a life of service. For most people, the energy that their sexual system generates provides for an enormous amount of productive work. When this energy is channeled into your career and in living your life as a fully devoted follower of Christ, the results can be astounding. I mentioned Mother Teresa earlier because she is an excellent example of what can be accomplished by someone who pours all her energy into serving God and others. Her life was not only incredibly important to millions in our world but also deeply meaningful and enriching for her personally.

I should point out that pursuing the service option doesn't necessarily mean a lifelong choice. If you are single today you need to embrace this option for now even if you intend to be married later. Channel your sexual energy into serving God and serving others. The service option even applies to those who are married but temporarily don't have access to legitimate sexual release (say you are away from your spouse, or your spouse is sick). You need to be in the habit of channeling that sexual energy into something constructive. Being married doesn't mean you never again have to deal with frustrated sexual longings.

Not an Option: Pornography

Pornography does not provide safe release for sexual tension. Over the last fifteen years this has become the most prevalent problem for people trying to control their sexual desire. Many men have told me their reasons for how they decided that pornography was okay while they were unmarried. The problem is there's never a good reason.

Many men believe that participating in pornography is a safe and painless way to deal with their sexual tension and keep from falling into having sexual relations with the women they are dating. I believe that God makes his position clear on this point. You do not have to live as a slave to evil desires:

> Therefore, since Christ suffered in his body, *arm yourselves also with the same attitude, because he who has suffered in his body is done with sin.* As a result, he does not live the rest of his earthly life for evil human desires, but rather for the

will of God. For you have spent enough time in the past doing what pagans choose to do—living in debauchery, lust, drunkenness, orgies, carousing and detestable idolatry. They think it strange that you do not plunge with them into the same flood of dissipation, and they heap abuse on you. But they will have to give account to him who is ready to judge the living and the dead. (1 Peter 4:1–5, emphasis added)

According to God's Word, you are not a slave to your sexual tension. If you are willing to "suffer a little while" (i.e., not give into lustful urges) then the temptation begins to lose its power and influence in your life to the point that you are done with sin. Any recovering addict will tell you that at first it feels like you will die, but later on, sanity is restored and you can easily replace such destructive habits with positive and appropriate things.

> You need to be in the habit of channeling that sexual energy into something constructive. Being married doesn't mean you never again have to deal with frustrated sexual longings.

Another reason I've often heard is that it is better to lust after a woman on paper or on film than to lust after the real woman in your life. The problem is that God says it is not acceptable to lust after any woman and that lusting in your heart is adultery. Lust is an issue primarily of the heart and mind, not primarily of the body. Hear what Jesus said on the subject:

You have heard that it was said, "Do not commit adultery." But I tell you that *anyone who looks at a woman lustfully has already committed adultery* with her in his heart. If your right eye causes you to sin, gouge it out and throw it away. It is better for you to lose one part of your body than for your whole body to be thrown into hell. And if your right hand causes you to sin, cut it off and throw it away. It is better for you to lose one part of your body than for your whole body to go into hell. (Matthew 5:27–30, emphasis added)

It will relieve you to know that Jesus' intent is not that you literally gouge out your eye or cut off your hand. But he is making the point that extreme effort must be made to stop catering to lust, even the "virtual" kind.

The last reason I've commonly heard is that pornography isn't hurting anyone and that after marriage it can be put aside because sex will be allowed, and lust will cease. There are several problems with this argument. First, pornography is a multibillion-dollar industry that has a devastating effect on society, especially on women and children. It is not victimless. In addition, any counselor will tell you that the number of people reporting a disabling addiction to pornography has skyrocketed in the last decade. Pornography is always about something deeper than mere sexual tension, and its addictive nature is very powerful. Unchecked, it will drive participants into more extreme and perverse behaviors in order to maintain the same level of excitement experienced during their first time with a simple magazine.

In essence, addiction to pornography is no different from a drug addiction. It works the same and causes equal damage to your life, especially in your ability to be fully intimate. It causes you to hide your emotional being from your spouse out of shame, and it robs a couple of the deeper levels of intimacy God intended for them. Finally, only a foolish man believes that lust that has been nurtured over the years, as a single man, will magically disappear once he is married and having sex. Pornography is ultimately an issue of the heart and mind and not just a physical exercise. To continually sin against your own body in this way causes deep wounds, and the "virtual" bonding that occurs with the women in pornography is just as disruptive to intimacy with your wife as having sex with a prostitute.

> Do you not know that your bodies are members of Christ himself? Shall I then take the members of Christ and unite them with a prostitute? Never! Do you not know that he who unites himself with a prostitute is one with her in body? For it is said, "The two will become one flesh." But he who unites himself with the Lord is one with him in spirit.
>
> Flee from sexual immorality. All other sins a man commits are outside his body, but he who sins sexually sins against his own body. Do you not know that your body is a temple of the Holy Spirit, who is in you, whom you have received from God? You are not your own; you were bought at a price. Therefore honor God with your body. (1 Corinthians 6:15–20)

My Story

Prior to my conversion to Jesus Christ, I was deeply involved with pornography. It started as a kid when I was exposed to Playboy magazine. Later, when I was a teenager and HBO new, movies that displayed simulated sex were suddenly available at the push of a button. In college it progressed to actual promiscuity as well as pornographic theaters. Much to my dismay and discomfort, twenty years later I still remember many of those images. I came to Christ in my late twenties and learned that I was not only sinning against God but also doing great damage to myself. I began a pattern of repeated sin and confession but never seemed to break the cycle of addiction.

After I was married and had even gone into the ministry, I realized that marriage really didn't eliminate lust even though I had a beautiful and willing wife. Freedom only came when I took the humbling and terrifying step I knew I had to take. I told my wife everything. I confessed to her, asked her forgiveness, and submitted myself to accountability with her and with a few trusted male friends. I shared my struggle with the people in my church and still do from the pulpit whenever I feel led by his Spirit. In time, God broke the power of the addiction as I learned that I was helpless without his strength. I also learned that he loved me even in my disgusting condition. His plan included my complete freedom from this and any other sin. He would complete what he had begun in me, and my job was to respond with faith, obedience, and humility.

Now, almost fifteen years later, I still need to depend on God and take advantage of accountability from friends. I can still be tempted and can struggle with thoughts and old images, but God has brought great healing into my soul. He has also enabled me and my wife to develop the multi-faceted intimacy that we always wanted—an intimacy that is spiritual, emotional, mental, and physical. I no longer hide in shame when I am with her. Much credit goes to my wife, because even though the knowledge of my sin hurt her deeply, she offered me grace and was committed to defeat this enemy of our relationship. Over time, she learned that it had nothing to do with any lack of beauty or desirability on her part. It was a broken place in my soul that only God could fix. We still have plenty of room to grow, but we are thankful for where we are and excited about continuing to reach new levels of intimacy even into our seventies and beyond.

Understanding the Divine Design of the Sexual Systems

When God created us male and female, he intentionally created us to be different. While men and women are equal in value they are not equivalent in design. These differences are wonderful and make life together far more exciting and challenging than it would be if we were the same. Not only are our body parts different, but our sexual systems work differently as well. When you understand this, it sets the stage for a divine relational dance in which the longer a couple is together the greater their potential for better sex. The reason so many couples today do not experience increasingly better sex is that they are either ignorant of God's design or are foolishly (perhaps stubbornly) not cooperating with it. Sexual arousal occurs in both sexes about every ninety minutes, but beyond that, men and women function quite differently. Let's take a look at these two marvels of God's design.

The Male Sexual System

How beautiful your sandaled feet, O prince's daughter! Your graceful legs are like jewels, the work of a craftsman's hands. Your navel is a rounded goblet that never lacks blended wine. Your waist is a mound of wheat encircled by lilies. Your breasts are like two fawns, twins of a gazelle. Your neck is like an ivory tower. Your eyes are the pools of Heshbon by the gate of Bath Rabbim. Your nose is like the tower of Lebanon looking toward Damascus. Your head crowns you like Mount Carmel. Your hair is like royal tapestry; the king is held captive by its tresses. How beautiful you are and how pleasing, O love, with your delights! Your stature is like that of the palm, and your breasts like clusters of fruit. I said, "I will climb the palm tree; I will take hold of its fruit." May your breasts be like the clusters of the vine, the fragrance of your breath like apples, and your mouth like the best wine. (Song of Solomon 7:1–9)

Sex for men is strongly visual and very physical—it starts at the physical level, and the emotional connection follows. Men have been wired by God with a hydraulic-type system. Sexual pleasure for men is linked directly to their reproductive system and their climax is limited to this system. In other words, at the simplest level, a man's sexual energy is driven by and centered in his reproductive organs. Visual and physical stimulation lead to sexual arousal and ultimately release. As long as there is no mental block or organic problem, the male will become sexually aroused and achieve release. *His initial and primary experience is a physical one.* A more emotional and relational response must be learned and can only be achieved in the context of a safe and exclusive relationship with a female with whom he can feel comfortable and competent.

Look back at the very erotic, visual, physical passage quoted from the Song of Solomon above. The narrator is telling about what he sees and every detail of the beloved's body is a turn-on. This is where sex starts for a man. He doesn't talk about feelings, but about the physical stimuli. Contrast that to this passage, also from Song of Solomon:

> My dove in the clefts of the rock, in the hiding places on the mountainside, show me your face, let me hear your voice; for your voice is sweet, and your face is lovely. Catch for us the foxes, the little foxes that ruin the vineyards, our vineyards that are in bloom. (Song of Solomon 2:14–15)

See how it's different? In this second passage, the man is beginning to grow in his comfort with the emotional and relational aspects of sexual intimacy as much as he exults in the physical pleasure from sex. His calling to his wife to come out of hiding, to hear her voice, and to catch the little foxes (i.e., problems in the relationship) is evidence that he is now desiring to connect in emotional and relational ways not previously mentioned.

The Female Sexual System

> My lover is mine and I am his; he browses among the lilies. Until the day breaks and the shadows flee, turn, my

lover, and be like a gazelle or like a young stag on the rugged hills. All night long on my bed I looked for the one my heart loves; I looked for him but did not find him. I will get up now and go about the city, through its streets and squares; I will search for the one my heart loves. So I looked for him but did not find him. The watchmen found me as they made their rounds in the city. "Have you seen the one my heart loves?" Scarcely had I passed them when I found the one my heart loves. (Song of Solomon 2:16–3:4)

I am my lover's and my lover is mine; he browses among the lilies. (Song of Solomon 6:3)

May the wine go straight to my lover, flowing gently over lips and teeth. I belong to my lover, and his desire is for me. Come, my lover, let us go to the countryside, let us spend the night in the villages. Let us go early to the vineyards to see if the vines have budded, if their blossoms have opened, and if the pomegranates are in bloom—there I will give you my love. The mandrakes send out their fragrance, and at our door is every delicacy, both new and old, that I have stored up for you, my lover. (Song of Solomon 7:9–13)

I am a wall, and my breasts are like towers. Thus I have become in his eyes like one bringing contentment. (Song of Solomon 8:10)

Women have been wired by God with a process-type system. Sexual pleasure for women is controlled by an internal clock involving a monthly cycle of hormones. A woman relates sexually via a psycho-social experience that allows multiple influences to affect her response—or lack there of. Her body may be well stimulated, but if her emotions are not equally engaged (or worse, shut down or wounded), she will find it difficult to experience sexual climax. Sexual response in a relational context is automatic for a woman. *Her initial and primary experience is an emotional one.* A more physical and uninhibited response must be learned and can only be achieved in the context of a safe and exclusive relationship with a male with whom she feels comfortable.

> A couple can develop a multifaceted intimacy that powerfully connects them spiritually, mentally, emotionally, and physically.

This progression of growing more comfortable with giving herself away and exulting in the physical aspects of sexual intimacy as much as the emotional aspects is obvious as you read Song of Solomon from beginning to end. The passages quoted above—all spoken in the woman's voice—depict this development from the emotional/relational ("I will search for the one whom my heart loves") to the physical/erotic ("I am a wall and my breasts are like towers").

The conclusion of the matter is that God has designed the sexual systems and gender wiring in such a way that, by following God's plan, a couple can develop a multifaceted intimacy that powerfully connects them spiritually, mentally, emotionally, and physically. This multidimensional relationship requires intentional effort, the security of a permanent commitment, time, a teachable spirit, and patience from both the husband and the wife. Over time, as the man gains freedom and maturity in relating emotionally, and the woman gains freedom and maturity in relating physically, the quality of the sexual experience increases with virtually no limitations. To put it another way, done biblically, a seventy-year-old couple who has been developing like this for forty years is truly having better sex than the twenty-five-year-old couple living next door. While the older couple may not have as much energy and stamina, the quality of their sexual encounters satisfies them completely—at multiple levels and in ways the younger couple has not even touched on yet. Does that kind of sex sound good to you? When you move up to Level Five, that's exactly what you have to look forward to.

To put it another way, done biblically, a seventy-year-old couple who has been developing like this for forty years is truly having better sex than the twenty-five-year-old couple living next door.

LEVEL FIVE

Dating after Saying I Do

When my brother got his MBA, our family treated him to a dinner cruise on Chesapeake Bay. A couple celebrating their seventieth wedding anniversary was seated nearby. The husband called over, "Masters degree–that's quite an accomplishment."

"So is seventy years of marriage," my brother replied.

"Yeah," the man whispered, "but you're done."

—Peggy Keane[16]

Level Five dating is what keeps a marriage healthy and vibrant. Many couples make the mistake of ignoring the need to date each other for life, and as a result, they find their love waning. At the extreme, a husband and wife see their kids leave the nest and look across the room at a spouse who seems like a stranger. It doesn't have to be this way, and it definitely shouldn't be this way for you. Whether the date is dinner and a movie, playing tennis, going to a concert, walking in the park, meeting another couple, or actually going to a mall, it is crucial that you continue the effort to date one another for life.

CHAPTER EIGHTEEN

Defining Level Five

*Dating Lie #18: Once you're married, the dating
and the fun are over.*

The Twelve Bonding Levels are not simply a checklist. You don't say, "Hand-to-hand contact—check. Now on to arm-to-shoulder—check. Now to arm-to-waist—check." In a strong relationship, a couple is constantly repeating those steps, which continually strengthens the bonds between them. Every date (and every day) starts at Bonding Stage One (eye-to-body) and progresses through the succeeding stages, perhaps going as far as Bonding Stage Twelve (genital-to-genital), or perhaps not. Let's look at an imaginary Level Five date, and you'll see what I mean.

It's early evening, and you both get ready for your night out on the town together. Throughout the day you thought about the playful hints, winks, and tender touches you gave each other over breakfast, playfully predicting a special time together later on. Those thoughts stirred your passion for each other and you eagerly looked forward to going out that night.

You leave the house and drive once again to the mall where you had your first date. Walking through the mall, you notice each other (eye-to-body), just as you did on that first date. Your eyes meet and dart away, and then come back again (eye-to-eye). You talk and laugh (voice-to-voice). First you hold hands (hand-to-hand), and then his arm slips around your shoulder (arm-to-shoulder). You enjoy stopping in the various stores on Levels One, Two, Three, and Four. The memories this stirs up are pleasurable and serve to remind you of your romantic journey together–the journey through the Dating Levels that brought you to marriage. They also help you regain perspective in the midst of the daily grind of life. His arm now goes around your waist and he pulls you close (arm-to-waist). Then you enjoy an unashamed but appropriate kiss as you sit together on a bench (face-to-face). You cuddle and brush the hair off each other's foreheads (hand-to-face). You gently rub his neck and shoulders as you sit watching people walk by and talking together (hand-to-body).

Taking your time to go through the first nine bonding stages provides joy, energy, and renewed feelings of love and romance, which make the journey through the last three stages that much more pleasurable. While an extra-special outing is needed occasionally, your regular dates do not have to cost a lot of money, which can especially be an issue after kids come into the picture.

You make your way up escalator after escalator until you are on the fifth floor. You stroll past the bank and get some money out of the automatic teller. There is no tension in this because you both have agreed to live on a budget. You have already planned to take this money and do something special with it tonight. With your arms around each other's waists, you walk into the lingerie store. For him, it is a little uncomfortable, but he is with you, so it is okay. You guide him to a rack to show him what you picked out earlier in the week. He blushes and laughs but gladly walks with you to the counter to pay for a piece of intimate apparel that is to be shared in private later. You go to your favorite restaurant and eat a pleasant meal and continue sharing your thoughts and talk about your day. As you leave the restaurant, you walk past the maternity shop. You both look into the window and notice a tiny pair of pants and wonder if they might be in your future.

After a day of flirting and an evening of connecting, you both are quite ready to get back home where the rest of your date will take place. Ultimately, you find yourself in the bedroom. The lights are low and you are unashamed; you know that God created this and that he delights when his children enjoy this great gift in marriage.

Your hands gently touch each other's bodies; gently stroking the face, the shoulders, an arm, and eventually the torso, especially the chest area. His mouth goes to your breast (Bonding Stage Ten). This is the first stage where you can experience feeling naked and unashamed with the opposite sex as in Genesis 2. The symbolism of the male being vulnerable and needy at the female's breast is undeniable. As a child, his mother's breast provided sustenance and nurture. Now, as he has left his mother and father and begun cleaving to his wife, he demonstrates by this act his willingness to seek such loving nurture only from you. And though his role is clearly to protect and provide for you, your equally important role of support and care is demonstrated in this act. This is profoundly meaningful both emotionally and spiritually, while also providing great physical pleasure.

After a while, there is a natural progression of touch to the lower regions, and your hands touch one another's genitals (Bonding Stage Eleven). At this point, naked, unashamed, comfortable in your respective roles, and secure in your official commitment, your sexual desires are free to be fully released and enjoyed. Your hands can now lovingly explore places on the body that were off limits before marriage. This level of touching provides exceptional physical pleasure and is the ultimate show of trust and physical vulnerability. The genitals are as easily injured as they are stimulated. Either pain or pleasure can result from their being touched, so the trustworthiness and intentions of your partner are of the utmost importance.

Finally, genital touches genital (Bonding Stage Twelve). By God's amazing design, a time-intensive process of five levels of dating has allowed twelve specific bonding stages to forge a relationship like none other. Because the relationship has been built with patience and care, good communication, trust, spiritual interaction, emotional intimacy, and a slow physical stoking of passion, this married couple can end their date with the ultimate of unions.

> Romance can only be nourished as the emotional and spiritual pursuit continues.

Afterward, you fall asleep in each other's arms. You know you will wake up once again to the real world of jobs, bills, and other responsibilities. But you also know that you will wake up next to the one person in the world who delights in you and gladly shares the challenges of each day—a person who knows you better than anyone except God himself. As you drift off, you remember that if you continue dating God's way for life, your relationship will just keep getting better. It will grow, mature, and change, all for the better. He stirs and you feel the warmth of his body next to yours. You draw closer still and welcome the sleep that quickly comes.

Touchstones at Level Five

Pay attention to the following things at Level Five:
- **Have a regular date night.** *Even after marriage, there are huge relational benefits in continuing to date one another. Romance can only be nourished as the emotional and spiritual pursuit continues. Reread the previous pages where I described our imaginary couple on a date after marriage. Notice how participating in activities that were similar to*

their premarital encounters stirred positive memories and helped set the tone of the evening. Too many couples allow the busyness of life to creep in, and before they realize it, they haven't been on a date in months, or sadly, years!

- **Stay out of a rut.** *People and relationships need to grow, even after marriage. You need to experience new things and nourish a sense of fun and adventure. Don't let your routines put you on autopilot. Most men will tell you that one of the most important things they look for in a woman is her ability to be his companion and friend—someone with whom to have fun. While this is also important to women, it seems to play an especially large role in the thinking of men. To accomplish this will require a team approach. Life will make you tired, and most couples find that, at any given time, one person is more up for adventure than the other. The one with the most energy in the moment needs to prayerfully encourage their spouse to shake it off and come play.*

> People and relationships need to grow, even after marriage. You need to experience new things and nourish a sense of fun and adventure. Don't let your routines put you on autopilot.

- **Respect the bonding stages after marriage.** *Men especially fall prey to the notion that once you're married it is perfectly okay to jump right into foreplay and intercourse, since it is now officially allowed. While occasionally this may be fine with both the husband and the wife, most of the time the opposite is true. Couples can and should continually progress through all the bonding stages if the relationship (and especially the sexual component of the relationship) is to remain healthy. When this is done, the wife feels loved, appreciated, and romanced, and the husband feels the excitement and anticipation that comes from the flirting that leads to the bedroom.*

May God bless you richly on your dating journey
and because of this book may you never have to say,
"We're Just Friends" or tell any other dating lies!

Notes

1. Donald Joy, *Bonding: Relationships in the Image of God* (Dallas: Word, 1985), 45–47. Donald Joy cites Desmond Morris, a secular zoologist who made these discoveries about human bonding. It may seem strange to borrow from an avowed secularist like Morris in a book about biblical dating, but his schema unintentionally affirms the Judeo-Christian blueprint found in Genesis 2, which instructs men to leave, cleave, and become one flesh with their wives.

2. The syphilis rate has increased five years in a row, and Chlamydia is up 5 percent over the previous year based on latest data from the Centers for Disease Control and Prevention, "Sexually Transmitted Disease Surveillance, 2008," (Atlanta, GA: U.S. Department of Health and Human Services, November 2009), http://www.cdc.gov/std/stats08/main.htm.

3. Albert Hsu, "Singleness: A Biblical Perspective," *Discipleship Journal* 108:36. www.logos.com.

4. David E. Bratt, "The Doctor is in with David E. Bratt, MD," *The Trinidad Guardian,* June (2003).

5. E. Mansell Pattison reports on his findings about the healthy "psychological kinship system" in *Pastor and Parish—A Systems Approach* (Philadelphia: Fortress Press, 1977), 18–19. My use of the concept of a Relational Safety Net is a metaphor I chose to interpret and apply one of the findings in his excellent and complex work.

6. Gordon MacDonald, *Restoring Your Spiritual Passion* (Nashville: Oliver Nelson, 1986), 176–77.

7. Dr. Neil Anderson's book *Victory Over the Darkness* (Ventura, CA: Regal Books, 1990) is an excellent resource to help you understand who you are in Christ.

8. I especially recommend Don Gabor, *How to Start a Conversation and Make Friends* (New York: Fireside, 2001).

9. Anderson, *Victory Over the Darkness*, 45–47.

10. C. S. Lewis, *The Four Loves* (New York: Harvest Books, 1960), 169.

11. Clint Eastwood, as quoted in about.com, http://marriage.about.com/gi/o.htm?zi=1/XJ&zTi=1&sdn=marriage&cdn=people&tm=137&f=20&su=p284.9.336.ip_&tt=11&bt=1&bts=1&zu=http%3A//imdb.com/name/nm0000142/bio.

12. For the purposes of this imaginary stroll through the mall, the "you" in the story will be the woman. If you're a man...well, you could use the practice seeing things from a woman's perspective.

13. George Gilder, *Men and Marriage* (Gretna, LA: Pelican, 1992).

14. Life Innovations, Inc., *Prepare/Enrich*, P.O. Box 190, Minneapolis, MN, 55440-0190.

15. David McCullough, *Truman* (New York: Simon & Schuster, 1992), 435; quoted in Robert J. Morgan: *Nelson's Complete Book of Stories, Illustrations, and Quotes* (Nashville: Thomas Nelson Publishers, 2000).

16. Submitted by Peggy Keane, Reader'sDigest.com, Laugh Lines, March 2007, www.rd.com/newsletters/humor/laughlinesMar2007.